Great American Writers
TWENTIETH CENTURY

EDITOR
R. BAIRD SHUMAN
University of Illinois

Arthur Miller • Marianne Moore
Toni Morrison • Alice Munro • Frank Norris
Joyce Carol Oates • Tim O'Brien • Flannery O'Connor

MARSHALL CAVENDISH
NEW YORK • TORONTO • LONDON • SYDNEY

Marshall Cavendish
99 White Plains Road
Tarrytown, New York 10591-9001

Website: www.marshallcavendish.com

© 2002 Marshall Cavendish Corporation

All rights reserved. No part of this book may be reproduced or utilized in any form or by any means electronic or mechanical, including photocopying, recording, or by an information storage and retrieval system, without prior written permission from the publisher and copyright holder.

Salem Press

    Editor: R. Baird Shuman
    Managing Editor: R. Kent Rasmussen

    Manuscript Editors: Heather Stratton
                             Lauren M. Mitchell
    Assistant Editor: Andrea Miller
    Research Supervisor: Jeffry Jensen
    Acquisitions Editor: Mark Rehn

Marshall Cavendish

    Project Editor: Marian Armstrong
    Editorial Director: Paul Bernabeo

Designer: Patrice Sheridan

Photo Research: Candlepants
                       Carousel Research
                       Linda Sykes Picture Research
                       Anne Burns Images

Indexing: AEIOU

Library of Congress Cataloging-in-Publication Data

Great American writers: twentieth century / R. Baird Shuman, editor.
    v. cm.
    Includes bibliographical references and indexes.
    Contents: v. 3. Agee-Bellow--v. 2. Benét-Cather--v. 3. Cormier-Dylan--v. 4. Eliot-Frost--v. 5. Gaines-Hinton--v. 6. Hughes-Lewis--v. 7. London-McNickle--v. 8. Miller-O'Connor--v. 9. O'Neill-Rich--v. 10. Salinger-Stein--v. 11. Steinbeck-Walker--v. 12. Welty-Zindel--v. 13. Index.
    ISBN 0-7614-7240-1 (set)—ISBN 0-7614-7248-7 (v. 8)
    1. American literature--20th century--Bio-bibliography--Dictionaries. 2. Authors, American--20th century--Biography--Dictionaries. 3. American literature--20th century--Dictionaries. I. Shuman, R. Baird (Robert Baird), 1929-

PS221.G74 2002
810.9'005'03
[B]   2001028461

Printed in Malaysia; bound in the United States

07 06 05 04 03 02   6 5 4 3 2 1

Volume 8 Illustration Credits
(a = above, b = below, l = left, r = right)

AP/Wide World Photos: 1126, 1128, 1130
Archive Photos/Getty Images: cover portrait of Marianne Moore, cover portrait of Toni Morrison, 1033, 1034, 1038, 1039, 1044, 1047, 1049
Bancroft Library, University of California, Berkeley: cover portrait of Frank Norris, 1085, 1086, 1087, 1092
Jerry Bauer: cover portrait of Alice Munro, cover portrait of Tim O'Brien, 1071, 1073, 1074, 1119, 1121
Nathan Benn/Corbis: 1122
Bridgeman Art Library International Ltd. 2001: 1125
Bridgeman Art Library International Ltd. 2001/ARS: 1124
Bridgeman Art Library International Ltd. 2001/The Maas Gallery, London: 1076
Larry Burrows/TimePix: 1131
Corbis: 1024, 1059, 1110, 1112, 1114, 1115
Corbis/Bettmann: 1133, 1149
Culver Pictures: 1014, 1019, 1097
Rebecca Davenport: 1144
Fine Art Museum of San Francisco, Gift of Mrs. Harold R. McKinnon and Mrs. Harry L. Brown, 1962.21: 1088
Collection of the Flint Institute of Arts, Gift of Mr. and Mrs. B. Morris Pelavin, 1971.43: 1067
© 1989 Leonard Freed/Magnum Photos, Inc.: 1108
Georgia Department of Archives and History: 1137, 1142
Giraudon/Art Resource, NY: 1072
Burt Glinn/Magnum Photos, Inc., © 2001: 1104
Bernard Gotfryd/Archive Photos: cover portrait of Joyce Carol Oates, 1103
The Granger Collection, New York: 1015
Darrell Gulin/Corbis: 1138
Cover of Flannery O'Connor's *A Good Man Is Hard to Find and Other Stories*, Harcourt Brace & Company: 1139
HarperCollins Publishers: 1143
Hirshhorn Museum and Sculpture Garden, Smithsonian Institution, Gift of Joseph H. Hirshhorn, 1966. Photograph by Lee Stalsworth: 1140
Historical Pictures/Stock Montage: 1099
Howard University Gallery of Art, Washington, D.C.: 1045, 1055
Hulton Getty Images: 1016, 1017
Special Collections, Ina Dillard Russell Library, Georgia College and State University: cover portrait of Flannery O'Connor, 1135, 1136
James Keyser/TimePix: 1056
Kobal Collection: 1096
Erich Lessing/Art Resource, NY: 1117
Prints and Photographs Collection, Library of Congress: 1053
Robert Maas/Corbis: 1054
Masterfile: 1041
The McClelland Collection: 1091
Minnesota Historical Society (neg. 55259): 1120
The Museum of Modern Art, New York. Blanchette Rockefeller Fund. Photograph © 2001 The Museum of Modern Art, New York: 1057
National Archives: 1061
National Gallery of Art, Washington, John Hay Whitney Collection, Photograph © 2001 Board of Trustees: 1109
The Newark Museum/Art Resource, NY: 1030
New Britain Museum of American Art. Harriet Russell Stanley Fund, © VAGA: 1146
New Jersey State Museum, © VAGA, Museum Purchase, FA1986.4.1: 1077
Dorothea Lange Collection. Oakland Museum of California, City of Oakland. Gift of Paul S. Taylor: 1081
Parrish Art Museum, Southampton, NY. Clark Collection, PAM #1958.5.7: 1083
Penguin Books: 1052, 1064, 1095, 1107
Photofest: 1020, 1021, 1023, 1026, 1027, 1029, 1051, 1094
Reprinted by permission of Vintage Books and Ballantine Books, Divisions of Random House, Inc.: 1075, 1080
Ken Regan/Buena Vista/Kobal Collection: 1063
Reynolda House, Museum of American Art, Winston-Salem, NC, Gift of Barbara B. Millhouse: 1141
William E. Sauro/New York Times Co./Archive Photos: 1104
Smithsonian American Art Museum, Washington, D.C./Art Resource, NY: 1065, 1079
SuperStock: 1036, 1042
Martha Swope/TimePix: cover portrait of Arthur Miller, 1013
W. Tenaillon/Corbis: 1106
Doris Ulmann, PH 38, Special Collections and University Archives, University of Oregon: 1069
UPI/Corbis-Bettmann: 1035
The Roland P. Murdock Collection, Wichita Art Museum, Wichita, Kansas: 1050
W. W. Norton & Company, Inc.: 1089

Contents

Arthur Miller   1013

Marianne Moore   1033

Toni Morrison   1049

Alice Munro   1071

Frank Norris   1085

Joyce Carol Oates   1103

Tim O'Brien   1119

Flannery O'Connor   1135

Volume Index   1151

Arthur Miller

BORN: October 17, 1915, New York, New York
IDENTIFICATION: Mid- to late twentieth-century playwright, novelist, and nonfiction writer best known for his Pulitzer Prize–winning play *Death of a Salesman* (1949) and his activities against the oppression of individual freedom.

Arthur Miller is considered one of the most important American playwrights of the World War II generation. He is most famous for *Death of a Salesman* and for his marriage to actress Marilyn Monroe in 1956. Many of his plays are frequently performed on Broadway and are studied in schools. In Miller's frank autobiography, *Timebends: A Life* (1987), he illustrates his lifelong fight for individual freedom. In 1956, he refused to cooperate with the House Un-American Activities Committee (HUAC) and was cited for contempt of Congress. As president of International PEN Club, Miller opposed governmental restraint of writers in Greece, refusing to allow the publication of his writing there.

The Writer's Life

Arthur Miller was born in New York City's Harlem on October 17, 1915, to Isadore Miller and Augusta Barnett Miller. His older brother, Kermit, became the fictionalized elder son in several Miller plays. His sister, Joan, born in 1921, became an actress, using the stage name "Joan Copeland."

The Early Years. After Miller's father suffered financial reverses in 1928, the family moved to Brooklyn. Miller was an indifferent student; however, his enthusiasm for literature was piqued when he read Fyodor Dostoyevski's *The Brothers Karamazov* (1879–1880) in 1933, which marked a turning point in his life. That year Miller was denied admission to the University of Michigan because of his spotty high school record.

The College Years. After working for his father for a year, Miller wrote directly to the admissions dean at the University of Michigan, saying that he had become "a much more serious fellow" since his high school graduation and that he sincerely desired admission. He entered the university and soon distinguished himself. Studying playwriting under Kenneth Rowe, he won two Jule and Avery Hopwood Awards for plays he wrote as class projects. In 1938, as a senior, he won the Theatre Guild National Award for "They Too Arise."

After College. After completing college, Miller went to New York City. In 1938 he worked with the Federal Theatre Project, a government-sponsored Depression-era program of the Works Progress Administration (WPA). When the project ended in 1940, Miller went on relief, continuing to write. On August 5, 1940, he married Mary Grace Slattery, a Michigan classmate, who worked at menial jobs, giving him time to write.

Miller continued writing during the years of World War II, producing radio plays and a novel, *Focus* (1945), about anti-Semitism. He flirted with communism, as many American intellectuals did. Two months after the birth of his first child, Jane, in 1944, his first Broadway play, *The Man Who Had All the Luck*, opened, closing after only six performances.

Miller can be seen as the tragedian of the middle class, placing center stage its unattainable hopes and myopic vision of an ideal family that have slowly soured through the years.

The Road to Fame. In January 1947, shortly before the birth of his second child, Robert, Miller's first successful play, *All My Sons*, opened on Broadway. Miller became much more involved in political affairs, lending his name to liberal causes. His radio plays and short stories were widely distributed.

In 1949 Miller emerged as one of the leading U.S. playwrights with the Broadway production of *Death of a Salesman*, a true American classic. In 1968 the one-millionth copy of the play was sold. It was revived on Broadway in 1999, a production that was heralded as a major theatrical event.

Death of a Salesman won both the New York Drama Critics Circle Award and the Pulitzer Prize for drama in 1949. Miller, publishing essays on drama and politics in *The New York Times*, was quickly becoming not only the most celebrated playwright in the United States but also one of the country's most strident advocates of individual freedom and human rights.

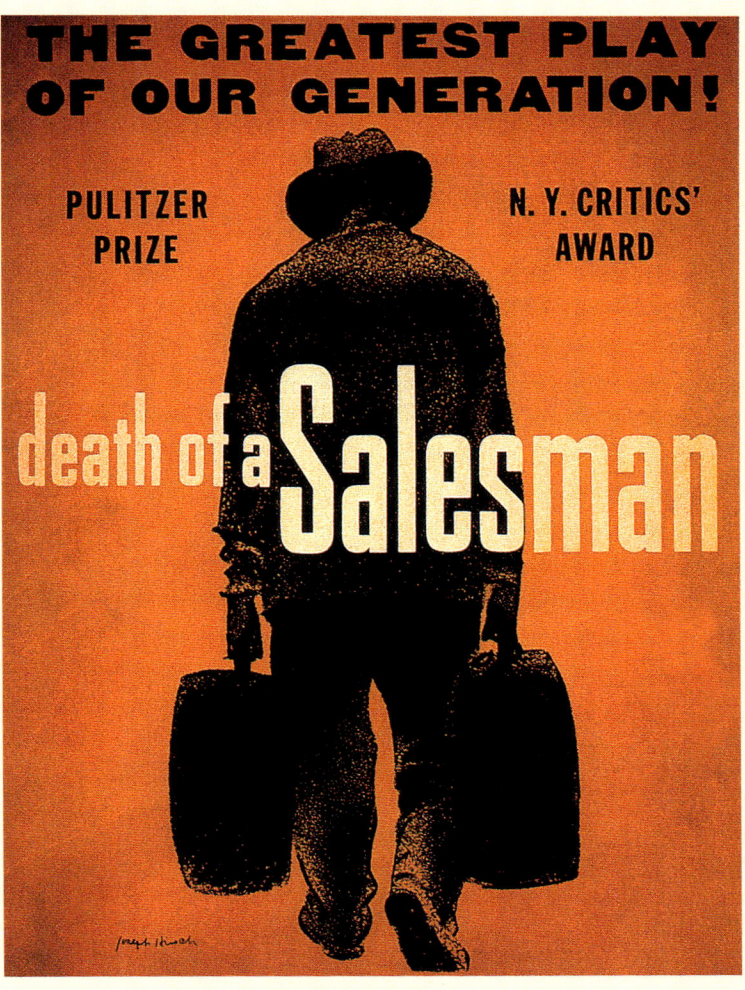

A famous image from a classic play, Joseph Hirsch's 1949 poster for *Death of a Salesman* shows Willy Loman slumping along with his sample cases, beaten down by too many years on the road.

Marilyn Monroe. Miller's rapid rise to celebrity had a significant effect on his personal life. In 1950 he met film star Marilyn Monroe, who was then married to baseball player Joe DiMaggio. By 1951 Miller frequently appeared at public functions without his wife. He mounted an adaptation of Henrik Ibsen's *An Enemy of the People* (1882) on Broadway in 1950 and wrote a screenplay, *The Hook* (1953). In that year his new play, *The Crucible*, opened on Broadway to mixed reviews.

In 1954 Monroe and DiMaggio were divorced. In the following year, when Miller and Monroe met again, they shared a mutual attraction. Miller divorced his wife in early 1956 and married Monroe in June of that year.

Contempt Conviction. Meanwhile, the United States was gripped by the threat of Cold-War communism. Beginning in the early 1950s, Senator Joseph McCarthy, fueled by public hysteria, ferreted out left-leaning people from the government and other areas, including the entertainment industry. Those suspects who would not cooperate in the witch-hunt and "name names" of other alleged communists were blacklisted.

Miller was associated with the political Left and knew communists, as many contemporary writers and artists did then. When the *New York Herald-Tribune* reported on Miller's political connections, the House Un-American Activities Committee focused on him. In June

The hot new couple of the moment, Miller and actress Marilyn Monroe pose for this 1956 photograph, one month after their wedding.

1956 the newly married Miller was summoned before a HUAC hearing and grilled about his connections. His refusal to name suspects resulted in his being cited for contempt of Congress. That, in turn, led to his conviction and blacklisting in 1957. In August of 1958 the U.S. Court of Appeals for the District of Columbia overturned Miller's contempt conviction.

Monroe's Deep Depression. Around this same period, Monroe suffered a miscarriage that plunged her into a depression from which she never recovered. In 1961 she obtained a Mexican divorce from Miller. Soon after, Miller married Ingeborg Morath. Before his divorce from Monroe, Miller had reshaped his short story, "The Misfits," into a screenplay for her. *The Misfits* was produced in 1961, with Monroe in the lead role.

Late in August 1962 Monroe committed suicide. The following year, Miller began work on *After the Fall* (1964), a deeply personal play inspired by Monroe's death. In it, the main character and narrator reflects bitterly on personal tragedy and political hypocrisy.

Miller as Activist. In March 1964 Miller went to Nuremberg, Germany, to cover the trials of Nazi war criminals for the *New York Herald-Tribune*. The experience led him to write *Incident at Vichy* (1964), a play set in France during the World War II German Occupation, which examines the nature of social responsibility. The following year, Miller was elected president of the International PEN Club, the leading international association for writers.

As president of PEN, Miller defended the rights of writers in countries whose oppressive regimes thwarted their writing. He refused to permit the publication of his work in Greece, where censorship had stilled the voices of many promising writers. He petitioned the Soviets to relax their ban on the works of Alexandr Solzhenitsyn, a Russian novelist who had been critical of the Stalinist regime. When Miller's term as president ended in 1969, he turned his attention to other human-rights matters, supporting a Massachusetts teacher who refused to say the pledge of allegiance in her classroom.

Miller's most productive period began in 1947 with the production of *All My Sons* and ended essentially with *The Price* in 1968. Miller became disenchanted with the way Broadway presented a number of his plays; most of his later openings were in venues outside New York.

The Writer's Work

While Arthur Miller is recognized as one of the most distinguished American playwrights of the twentieth century, his reputation is based largely on the great commercial success he attained very early in his career. His fame and distinction rests on two early plays, *Death of a Salesman* and *The Crucible*.

Early Success. Miller began writing plays before his twentieth birthday and won the Jule and Avery Hopwood Award in both 1936 and 1937 for two of his student plays. Miller graduated from the University of Michigan in 1938 and went to New York City, where he worked briefly for the Federal Theatre Project, a program sponsored by the government's Works Progress Administration. He wrote thirty-minute radio plays for CBS and NBC. Although frustrated by the artistic restrictions that the networks and their advertisers imposed, he developed focus and compression through this writing, lessons that later served him well.

Political Voice. From 1941 to 1945, Miller wrote propagandistic plays in support of the fight against fascism, among them "The Four Freedoms," "The Half-Bridge," and *That They May Win* (1944). In 1945 he published a novel, *Focus*, decrying anti-Semitism. Miller's first Broadway play, *The Man Who Had All the Luck*, examined the success of its main character, David Frieber, who struggles to understand his good fortune. The play closed after six performances but won a Theatre Guild National Award.

Miller's first successful play, *All My Sons*, which ran for 328 performances, deals with father-son relationships, one of his recurring topics. Joe Keller, a manufacturer of airplane cylinders, ships a batch of them out of his plant, hiding the fact that they are defective. The hairline cracks in the cylinders result in many plane crashes and deaths. Joe's own son, Larry, is a pilot missing in action. It finally is revealed that Larry, discovering his father's culpability, has committed suicide by crashing his plane. Keller, acknowledging his guilt, shoots himself. The play won the New York Critics Circle Drama Award.

Broadway Debuts. Miller's most successful play is *Death of a Salesman*; it won Miller a Pulitzer Prize, among many other awards. The play opened in 1949 and ran for 742 performances, with frequent revivals on Broadway. In 1968 the one-millionth copy of *Death of a Salesman* was sold. The basic idea for the play first sur-

Photographer Charles Hewitt snapped this photo of Miller on October 20, 1956. Though success found Miller at a relatively young age, the budding playwright still served a long apprenticeship as a writer. Despite the restriction of working in radio, Miller learned invaluable lessons in pacing and dramatic structure.

HIGHLIGHTS IN MILLER'S LIFE

1915 Arthur Miller is born in New York City on October 17.
1928 Moves to Brooklyn with his family.
1933 Graduates from Abraham Lincoln High School.
1934 Enters the University of Michigan, where two of his plays win Jule and Avery Hopwood Awards.
1938 Wins Theater Guild National Award for "They Too Arise."
1938–1939 Works in New York City with Federal Theatre Project.
1940 Marries Mary Grace Slattery.
1942 Writes "The Four Freedoms," an unpublished radio play.
1944 First Broadway production, *The Man Who Had All the Luck*, closes after six performances; daughter Jane is born.
1945 Miller publishes first novel, *Focus*; attacks poet Ezra Pound for profascist activities.
1947 *All My Sons* opens on Broadway; son Robert is born.
1949 *Death of a Salesman* opens on Broadway, garnering New York Drama Critics Circle Award and Pulitzer Prize.
1950 Miller meets Marilyn Monroe; mounts adaptation of Henrik Ibsen's *An Enemy of the People* on Broadway.
1953 *The Crucible* opens on Broadway.
1955 Miller is attacked in the *New York Herald-Tribune* as a communist sympathizer.
1956 Divorces Slattery; marries Monroe; appears before House Un-American Activities Committee.
1957 Is convicted of contempt of Congress and is blacklisted; writes short story "The Misfits."
1958 Miller's contempt conviction is overturned by U.S. Court of Appeals.
1959 Receives Gold Medal for Drama from the National Institute of Arts and Letters.
1961 Miller is divorced by Monroe.
1962 Marries Ingeborg Morath; Monroe commits suicide.
1964 Miller attends Nazi war trials in Germany; publishes *Incident at Vichy*.
1965 Is elected president of the International PEN Club.
1968 Sells one-millionth copy of *Death of a Salesman*; is delegate to Democratic National Convention.
1969 Protests Greece's suppression of writers by not permitting publication of his work there; publishes nonfiction *In Russia*.
1972 Produces *The Creation of the World and Other Business*; is delegate to Democratic National Convention.
1983 Directs production of *Death of a Salesman* in China.
1984 Publishes *"Salesman" in Beijing*; revives *Death of a Salesman* on Broadway.
1987 Publishes autobiography, *Timebends: A Life*.

The famed theater and film director Elia Kazan (left) was at the helm of *Death of a Salesman*'s long and successful run.

faced in Miller's short story, "In Memorium" [sic], which he wrote at the age of seventeen. The theme reiterates his concern with father-son relationships. A delusional Willy Loman, who has imbued his two sons with an untenable value system, finds his world collapsing around him and crashes his car so that he can die and leave his life-insurance money to his family.

Miller's version of Henrik Ibsen's *An Enemy of the People* ran for thirty-six Broadway performances in 1950 and was published the following year. Then Miller exercised his interests in social and political injustice to write *The Crucible*, based on the 1692 witch trials in Salem, Massachusetts, which resulted in the hangings of nineteen people. The play opened on Broadway in 1953.

McCarthy and Monroe. Although it has become an American classic, *The Crucible* was perhaps too sensitive a topic for widespread public acceptance during the rise of McCarthyism in the United States. Miller himself was under the scrutiny of the House Un-American Activities Committee. In 1954 he was denied a passport to go to Brussels to receive an award for the play.

Following his marriage to Marilyn Monroe, Miller wrote "The Misfits," first as a short story that appeared in *Esquire*. He then later transformed it into a screenplay as a film vehicle for Monroe. In 1961 it was published as a novel. Monroe's suicide in 1962 following her divorce from Miller resulted in his writing his most personal play, *After the Fall*, produced in 1964.

Miller went to Nuremberg, Germany, in March 1964 to cover the Nazi war criminal trials for the *New York Herald-Tribune* as a special commentator. This experience inspired his play *Incident at Vichy*, which examines how personal integrity can be compromised by societal pressures. Miller's last commercially successful play was *The Price*, which ran on Broadway for 425 performances in 1968. His later plays, at his insistence, usually opened outside New York. *The Creation of the World and Other Business* had a run of twenty performances in 1972. Such later plays as *The Archbishop's Ceiling* (1984), *Danger: Memory!* (1986), and *The American Clock* (1980) were badly received.

Major Themes. Miller wrote most effectively about families, exploring the tensions created when individuals facing moral dilemmas are subjected to unrelenting social pressures. His portrayal of father-son relationships in *All My Sons* examines the tensions between Joe Keller and his sons, Chris and Larry. *Death of a Salesman* focuses not only on Willy Loman's relations with his sons, Happy and Biff, but also on the relationship between Willy's neighbor, Charley, and his son, Bernard.

McCarthyism and the repressive environment of the 1950s heightened Miller's need to write about how political expediency can jeopardize personal integrity. His political activism is reflected poignantly in his later plays, particularly in *The Crucible*.

Miller and Monroe on the set of *The Misfits*. It was to mark the end of their five-year marriage and to be the troubled actress's final film.

BIBLIOGRAPHY

Bigsby, Christopher, ed. *Arthur Miller and Company*. London: Methuen, 1990.

Bloom, Harold, ed. *Arthur Miller*. New York: Chelsea House, 1987.

Centola, Stephen R., ed. *The Achievement of Arthur Miller: New Essays*. Dallas, Tex.: Northouse, 1994.

———, ed. *Arthur Miller in Conversation*. Dallas, Tex.: Northouse, 1993.

Martin, Robert A., ed. *Arthur Miller: New Perspectives*. Englewood Cliffs, N.J.: Prentice-Hall, 1982.

Miller, Arthur. *Timebends: A Life*. New York: Penguin, 1995.

Moss, Leonard. *Arthur Miller*. Rev. ed. Boston: Twayne Publishers, 1980.

Roudané, Matthew C., ed. *Approaches to Teaching Miller's "Death of a Salesman."* New York: Modern Language Association, 1995.

Savran, David. *Communists, Cowboys, and Queers: The Politics of Masculinity in the Work of Arthur Miller and Tennessee Williams*. Minneapolis: University of Minnesota Press, 1992.

Schlueter, June, and James K. Flanagan. *Arthur Miller*. New York: Frederick Ungar, 1987.

SOME INSPIRATIONS BEHIND MILLER'S WORK

A turning point came for Arthur Miller during his last year in high school: He read Fyodor Dostoyevski's *Bratya Karamazovy* (1879–1880; *The Brothers Karamazov*, 1912). His indifferent high school record had originally prevented his admission to the University of Michigan, but he persisted and was admitted a year after his high school graduation.

At the university, he studied playwriting with Kenneth Rowe and also read widely in drama, particularly the plays of Henrik Ibsen and Eugene O'Neill. The unprecedented success of Clifford Odets's *Waiting for Lefty*, *Awake and Sing*, and *Paradise Lost*, all produced in 1935, also piqued his interest in playwriting.

The heavily interventionist New Deal programs of President Franklin D. Roosevelt, which were designed to provide social and economic relief from the ravages of the Great Depression, helped to shape Miller's political philosophy, as did his participation in the Federal Theatre Project in the late 1930s.

In 1950 Miller met Marilyn Monroe, whom he married in 1956 after divorcing his first wife. Miller and Monroe divorced in 1961, and shortly afterward Monroe committed suicide. Miller was shattered by her death, and his experience with her led him to write *After the Fall*.

Reader's Guide to Major Works

ALL MY SONS

Genre: Drama
Subgenre: Social realism
Published: New York, 1947
Time period: 1940s
Setting: Keller family's backyard

Themes and Issues. *All My Sons*, Arthur Miller's first Broadway success, is much influenced by the drama of Henrik Ibsen. In this play, Miller observes the classical dramatic unities of time and place, unfolding a complex story in a single August afternoon in the Kellers' backyard. The play's fundamental concern, as in many of Miller's subsequent plays, is with the individual's relation to the broader society and the revelation of the inner self in opposition to the person everyone sees. The basic conflict is between the integrity and identity of the individual and the value system of American society. As in later Miller plays, the father-son relationship is central to the development of the play's thematic content.

The Plot. Joe Keller is an affluent manufacturer of airplane parts, whose business profited greatly from World War II. Like many of Ibsen's characters, however, Joe Keller is haunted by his past. He was convicted of knowingly permitting cylinder heads with hairline cracks to leave his factory and be installed in P-40 planes, some of which crashed, resulting in the

Burt Lancaster, Mady Christians, and Edward G. Robinson in a scene from the 1948 film version of *All My Sons*. In the Keller family, guilt is the legacy passed through the generations.

deaths of twenty-one pilots. Joe beat his conviction when, on appeal, he shifted the blame to his former business partner, who is now serving time in prison as a consequence.

Joe's son, Larry, a pilot in the war, has been missing in action for three years. His brother Chris now reveals that he intends to marry Ann Deever, Larry's fiancé and the daughter of Joe's imprisoned ex-partner. Joe's wife, Kate, who is unwilling to admit that Larry might be dead, stands adamantly against the marriage of Chris and Ann.

In the course of the play, Chris, who had staunchly defended Joe during his trials, discovers his father's unquestionable guilt. All three Kellers become aware that Larry died in the war by purposely crashing his plane, committing suicide out of shame for his father's disgraceful acts. Joe's obvious guilt in the charge of involuntary manslaughter is now out in the open.

What follows is, in essence, a trial held in the Kellers' backyard. Chris assumes a Christ-like role, serving as both prosecutor and judge. Joe says, "Chris, you can't be a Jesus in this world," but Chris will not accept this admonition. During these informal, backyard proceedings, Joe finally realizes that there are more important things in life than providing a secure and comfortable life for his family.

Earlier he says of Chris, "I'm his father and he's my son and if there's something bigger than that I'll put a bullet in my head." Then Chris, confronting his father, asks the cogent question posed directly or indirectly in most of Miller's plays, "Who the hell are you?" Joe acknowledges to himself that the twenty-one downed P-40 pilots were, indeed, "all my sons." He answers Chris's question about his identity by leaving the stage and firing a bullet into his head.

Analysis. Following the classical rules of structure, Miller creates a complex situation in which the play's three characters all confront the ghosts they have refused to acknowledge in the past. Chris undergoes a painful awakening as he comes to realize who his father really is.

Kate is forced not only to acknowledge Larry's death but also to acknowledge her husband's complicity in bringing it about.

The Kellers' family ties had simultaneously unified them with and isolated them from the ethical values of their society. These ties are rent asunder by Chris's question, "Who the hell are you?" In response, the Kellers must now accept the fact that a relatedness must exist between the individual and society.

SOURCES FOR FURTHER STUDY

Bigsby, Christopher, ed. *Arthur Miller and Company*. London: Methuen, 1990.

Bloom, Harold, ed. *Arthur Miller*. New York: Chelsea House, 1987.

Miller, Arthur. *Timebends: A Life*. New York: Penguin, 1995.

Schlueter, June, and James K. Flanagan. *Arthur Miller*. New York: Frederick Ungar, 1987.

THE CRUCIBLE

Genre: Drama
Subgenre: Social criticism
Published: New York, 1953
Time period: 1692
Setting: Salem, Massachusetts

Themes and Issues. The community of Salem, Massachusetts, in 1692 was being torn apart from within by the Salem witch trials, which resulted in the executions of a number of people who were falsely accused of witchcraft. In the 1950s, when Miller wrote *The Crucible*, the United States was in a similar hysteria over the witch hunts of Senator Joseph McCarthy and others investigating individuals whom they suspected of past communist associations or communist leanings. The communist hunters accused members of the government as well as writers, teachers, and intellectuals, and demanded compliance to avoid implication of guilt.

In both Salem and Washington, D.C., the flames of distrust were fueled by suspicion and false accusation. Those in Salem who refused to confess to accusations of witchcraft were judged guilty and hanged. In Washington,

Actress Winona Ryder is backed against a tree by actor Daniel Day-Lewis in a confrontation from the 1996 film adaptation of *The Crucible*. Miller's play served as a warning, an example drawn from history in which fear, gullibility, and self-protection at any price collide to destroy a community's sense of unity.

those who maintained silence when brought before the House Un-American Activities Committee (HUAC) of Congress were deemed guilty. Miller stalwartly refused to give Congress the information its minions sought. In 1957, he was convicted of contempt of Congress, a charge that was reversed the following year by the U.S. Court of Appeals.

Clearly, *The Crucible* is an allegory intended to reflect what was happening in American politics during the McCarthy era. The play's conflict is one of people against an unjust, irrational, and at times hysterical society.

The Plot. *The Crucible*, set in Salem in 1692, is superficially the story of John and Elizabeth Proctor during the witchcraft trials. The precipitating event happens when the Reverend Parris catches a group of hysterical young girls committing a prank in the woods. The girls hope to avoid punishment by shifting suspicion away from themselves, and they claim to have been bewitched by Tituba, a black servant.

A climate of distrust begins to destroy the town, where some people are weak enough to cast unjustified suspicion on their neighbors in order to save their own reputations and to protect their places in the community. John Proctor, suspected of a dalliance with Abigail, one of the hysterical girls, is an obvious scapegoat, as is Tituba, who, simply by being black, is suspect in a town overcome by fear of strangers and anything extraordinary.

Even wives are pitted against husbands: When John Proctor most needs Elizabeth's support and testimony as to his innocence, she chooses to save herself. In so doing, she paves the way for John's condemnation and eventual execution. Proctor can save himself only by confessing to acts he did not commit. He, like Miller before the HUAC, refuses to give the false testimony that might save him but would implicate his friends and compromise his

Joseph McCarthy muffles microphones with his hands while being briefed by the attorney Roy Cohn during a hearing in 1954. The senator's own private witch-hunt initiated a time of suppression and paranoia. Reputations were marred, and careers were destroyed. Not even Miller escaped the mudslinging.

ideals. He declares that he cannot "live without [his] name." As a result of his admirable stand, he is hanged, leaving his wife and children in a society destroying itself from within.

Analysis. It is impossible to discuss *The Crucible* outside of the political and social context of the United States during the early 1950s. The anticommunist hysteria of the time was pervasive, spurred on by the unwarranted and unproved accusations of an ambitious, power-hungry senator. When Arthur Miller fell victim to this hysteria, he realized that the stage was the perfect venue for exposing the absurdity and imminent danger to society of the HUAC hearings.

The Salem witch trials grew out of the overpowering self-righteousness of Salem's most ignorant and unthinking citizens. Reason could not prevail in the narrow religious atmosphere that characterized seventeenth-century Puritan Salem. There, power was in the hands of those least able to use it wisely.

In *The Crucible*, Arthur Miller's political activism and heroic resistance to oppression reach their acme. To produce such a play at a time when the United States was under the grip of a rampant and despotic Congress was a singular act of bravery on the part of a playwright whose most prominent loyalty was to the ideals of individual integrity in the face of dire threats. *The Crucible* will maintain its relevance as long as unbridled power runs rampant in any part of the world.

SOURCES FOR FURTHER STUDY

Bloom, Harold, ed. *The Crucible*. Philadelphia: Chelsea House, 1999.

Dukore, Bernard F. *"Death of a Salesman" and "The Crucible."* Atlantic Highlands, N.J.: Humanities Press International, 1989.

Martine, James J. *The Crucible: Politics, Property, and Pretense*. New York: Twayne Publishers, 1993.

Partridge, C. J. *The Crucible*. Oxford, England: Oxford University Press, 1971.

PLAYS

- 1944 That They May Win (one act)
- 1944 The Man Who Had All the Luck
- 1947 All My Sons
- 1949 Death of a Salesman
- 1950 An Enemy of the People (adaptation of Henrik Ibsen's drama)
- 1953 The Crucible
- 1955 A Memory of Two Mondays
- 1955 A View from the Bridge (one-act version)
- 1956 A View from the Bridge (two-act version)
- 1957 Collected Plays
- 1964 After the Fall
- 1964 Incident at Vichy
- 1968 The Price
- 1970 Fame
- 1972 The Creation of the World and Other Business
- 1974 Up from Paradise (musical version of The Creation of the World and Other Business)
- 1980 The American Clock
- 1982 Some Kind of Love Story (one act)
- 1982 Elegy for a Lady (one act)
- 1984 The Archbishop's Ceiling
- 1986 Danger: Memory! (two one-act plays, Clara and I Can't Remember Anything)
- 1991 The Ride down Mt. Morgan
- 1993 The Last Yankee
- 1994 Broken Glass

RADIO PLAYS

- 1941 The Pussycat and the Expert Plumber Who Was an Honest Man; William Ireland's Confession
- 1944 "The Four Freedoms" (unpublished)
- 1945 Grandpa and the Statue
- 1947 The Story of Gus
- 1947 The Guardsman (radio adaptation of Ferenc Molnar's play)
- 1947 Three Men on a Horse (radio adaptation of George Abbott's and John Cecil Holm's script)

SCREENPLAYS

- 1961 The Misfits
- 1990 Everybody Wins

LONG FICTION

- 1945 Focus
- 1961 The Misfits
- 1995 Homely Girl, A Life, and Other Stories

SHORT FICTION

- 1967 I Don't Need You Any More

NONFICTION

- 1944 Situation Normal
- 1969 In Russia (photo essay; with Ingeborg Morath)
- 1977 In the Country (photo essay; with Morath)
- 1978 The Theater Essays of Arthur Miller, ed. Robert A. Martin
- 1979 Chinese Encounters (photo essay; with Morath)
- 1984 "Salesman" in Beijing
- 1987 Conversations with Arthur Miller, ed. Matthew C. Roudané
- 1987 Spain
- 1987 Timebends: A Life
- 1990 Arthur Miller and Company, ed. Christopher Bigsby

DEATH OF A SALESMAN

Genre: Drama
Subgenre: Realism
Published: New York, 1949
Time period: 1940s
Setting: Brooklyn, New York

Themes and Issues. *Death of a Salesman* presents the downfall of a deluded shoe salesman, who creates a fantasy world in which he insulates himself from life's realities. More than the personal tragedy of one man, this play concerns failures in modern society.

Willy Loman swallows the bait that American society dangles before him. He reveres material success but has not enjoyed it. In a delusional scene involving his brother Ben, he convinces himself that he could have succeeded if he had gone into business with Ben when he had the opportunity. Ben disappeared into the jungle and emerged a rich man four years later. Willy exudes unwarranted optimism. Only by believing his own lies can he face life, but these lies betray him. The collapse of his value system shatters his ideals.

In the 1978 film version of *Death of a Salesman*, Ben, played by Royal Beal, is a shadowy figure who returns from the dead to plague the thoughts of Willy Loman, portrayed by Frederic March.

unceremoniously, his sons have no future. The theme of denial permeates the play. Willy is the victim of his own deceptions, from which the only escape seems to be suicide, the option he finally accepts.

The Plot. Willy Loman has spent his life as a traveling shoe salesman. At sixty-three years of age, he is having difficulty selling shoes on the road. He sets out for New England but soon returns home, having two or three times run his car off the road. He can no longer drive safely.

Willy's most revered quality is that he is well liked. He knows that Howard, son of the former head of the shoe company and his father's successor, will find a place for him in the New York office. Buoyed by unrealistic optimism, he asks, finally begs, Howard for an office job.

Biff, on the same day, seeks a loan from the owner of the sporting goods store who idolized him when he was a football star. He believes that this loan will set him and Happy up in business. Willy and the two sons plan a victory celebration in a restaurant at the end of this auspicious day. The celebration turns into a dirge: Willy is dismissed without sufficient means to sustain himself and his wife, Linda. Biff's request for a loan is rejected by the man who once worshiped him but now fails to recognize him. Completely disheartened, Biff steals the man's fountain pen and flees.

Willy's life unravels precipitously in the restaurant scene with his sons, Happy and Biff. Neither Happy nor Biff has amounted to anything in life, despite Biff's prodigious beginning as his high school's best football player. In Willy's eyes, a world of opportunity was open to Biff. Now in his mid-thirties, Biff has drifted from one dead-end job to another. He steals, is caught, and is jailed, and his reputation is irreparably tarnished.

Willy pins his hopes on his boys. It now becomes clear that, as his own career is ending

Biff's petty thievery is fundamental to the play. Willy had always encouraged his sons to

Brian Dennehy, Ron Eldard, Ted Koch, and Elizabeth Franz (left to right) starred in the successful 2000 Broadway revival of *Death of a Salesman*.

ignore small transgressions. As adolescents, they stole lumber, which Willy rationalized the construction company would never miss, to help Willy build a front stoop. When Biff was offered athletic scholarships, he could not accept them because he had failed mathematics and would not graduate. Biff went to Boston, where Willy was on a sales trip, to get Willy to talk his mathematics teacher into changing his grade. In the Boston hotel, Biff discovered his father in bed with a woman, which forever changes the father-son relationship.

Before the restaurant scene, Willy, dismissed by Howard, approaches his longtime friend and neighbor, Charley, for a loan. Charley's son, Bernard, in his father's office when Willy arrives, is preparing to plead a case before the Supreme Court. Willy cannot understand how Bernard, who once vied for the honor of carrying Biff's shoulder guards onto Ebbets Field, has succeeded, because Bernard, although liked, was not *well* liked.

At the restaurant, Happy picks up two girls. He and Biff leave, abandoning their distraught father. Willy, shattered and humiliated, limps home. The next morning, Linda orders both boys out of the house, but not before Biff upbraids his father, calling him a fool and a dreamer. However, when Biff starts to weep, Willy realizes that Biff loves him.

Willy, who has life insurance worth twenty thousand dollars, thinks that this money can buy Biff and Happy a new beginning. He drives away in his car. The final scene is Willy's funeral, attended only by Linda, her sons, and Charley, who explains to Biff that salesmen need dreams if they are to succeed. Linda places a flower on Willy's fresh grave.

Analysis. *Death of a Salesman* focuses on middle-class American values. Willy is not evil, but he is fundamentally dishonest. His dishonesty is in his inability to accept the realities of his own existence. He has carefully constructed unrealistic dreams of what his life might have been and of what his sons' lives will be. Biff and Happy are like their father. Nearing middle age, they are still incapable of attaining full maturity. The tragedy of Willy Loman is his inability to accept himself and his position in society. Biff and Happy are continuations of this tragedy.

SOURCES FOR FURTHER STUDY

Altena, I., and A. M. Aylwin. *Notes on Arthur Miller's "Death of a Salesman."* London: Methuen, 1976.

Bloom, Harold, ed. *Arthur Miller's "Death of a Salesman."* New York: Chelsea House, 1988.

Meserve, Walter J., ed. *The Merrill Studies in "Death of a Salesman."* Columbus, Ohio: Merrill, 1972.

Roudane, Matthew C., ed. *Approaches to Teaching Miller's "Death of a Salesman."* New York: Modern Language Association, 1995.

Other Works

AFTER THE FALL (1964). Written shortly after Marilyn Monroe's suicide in 1962, *After the Fall* consists of more than forty nonsequential episodes from the memories of Quentin, a twice-divorced attorney in his forties. The play was commissioned as the opening production of the new Lincoln Center Repertory Company in New York City.

Quentin's experiences—his parents' difficulties during the Great Depression, his first marriage to Louise, his isolation during investigations of his political activities, his relationship with the innocent Maggie and her disintegration and death, and the shadow of Nazi concentration camps—parallel many of Arthur Miller's personal experiences. Hence, the play was shunned by some critics as being too subjective.

The stage, bare except for one chair, is dominated on its highest level by the "blasted stone tower of a German concentration camp." Its wide lookout windows stare like eyes over the set. From the tower bent metal rods stick out like tentacles.

In both method of presentation and structure of the set, Miller's expressionism is more pervasive than in any of his earlier writing. He employed elements of expressionism in *Death of a Salesman*, in the memory scenes involving Willy's brother Ben and Willy's liaison in Boston, as he did in the garden setting in *All My Sons*.

After the Fall, however, is Miller's most expressionistic play. In it the results of his earlier dramatic experimentation with expressionism reached full fruition. In this play, Quentin is poised between his association with two women, the recently dead Maggie and Holga, a concentration-camp survivor. He is haunted by Ibsen-like ghosts, as are the characters in *All My Sons* and *Death of a Salesman*.

The fall in Miller's title refers to the loss of innocence, the fall presented in the biblical Garden of Eden. Quentin is a modern Adam, but he also often resembles the biblical Cain. Throughout the play, the looming concentration camp tower makes its own statement about the loss of innocence during a century in which corruption, distrust, and persecution have become dominant factors.

THE PRICE (1968). In this play, Miller juxtaposes two brothers with opposing value systems. Each brother carries a burden from the past, reawakened by his coming to the Manhattan brownstone, about to be demolished, where possessions of the men's dead parents, the Franzes, are warehoused.

The sons, Victor and Walter, followed very different careers. When the father was ruined by the stock-market crash of 1929, Walter turned his back on his parents and struggled to put himself through medical school. Now a surgeon, he is divorced, displeased with his own sons, and sufficiently disturbed to have been hospitalized for a mental breakdown. Victor, the younger son, stood by his parents, foregoing a college education and becoming a policeman.

Miller soon reveals that although the elder Franz appeared impoverished, he had secreted away enough money to make him feel secure. Walter had suspected as much, but Victor was unaware of this deception, making what was actually an unnecessary sacrifice to give his parents money. Victor, apprised by Walter of their father's duplicity, is not bitter.

He insists that the proceeds from the sale of their parents' possessions be divided equally between him and his brother, despite Victor's great economic sacrifices and Walter's current affluence. Rather than insisting that Victor take everything, Walter proposes that he give the

In *The Price*, Miller slightly alters his formula. Two brothers are unable to confront their troubled relationship with their father, plagued with issues that his death leaves unresolved. The title of the play bears metaphoric, ironic weight, not only referring to money but the personal and emotional cost to the siblings, the loss of dignity, and the loss of years. Victor, played by actor Pat Hingle (left), strikes up a deal with the junk dealer, portrayed by Harold Gary, in this stage scene from *The Price*.

In his 1922 oil and tempera painting *The Voice of the City of New York Interpreted: The Bridge*, Joseph Stella presents the hulking symbol of the Brooklyn Bridge as a filter for the promise of a better life that lies beyond. For the two Italian immigrants in *A View from the Bridge*, the hope of a new start in America is unwittingly compromised. In the play, Miller plays with the notion of vision and differing viewpoints of moral, responsible behavior.

possessions to the Salvation Army and take a tax deduction, which he will share with Victor.

Victor considers this proposal, but he has made a commitment to the junk dealer on which he will not renege. Walter offers Victor a job in hospital administration. This assuages Walter's conscience for having refused years ago to lend Victor five hundred dollars that would have enabled him to attend college.

In this play, in which Miller again focuses on father-son relationships, two value systems are juxtaposed. Victor clearly is morally superior to Walter, who conforms more nearly to common notions of success.

A VIEW FROM THE BRIDGE (1955, 1956). In *A View from the Bridge*, Miller deals, as in many other plays, with the questions of loyalty and universal ethics versus personal values. Eddie Carbone is a longshoreman who, with his wife, Bea, has raised his niece, Catherine, since she was a child. Complications set in when two remote relatives of Catherine arrive from Sicily. They are illegal immigrants whom Eddie has vowed to look after.

When Catherine falls in love with the younger immigrant, Rodopho, Eddie is driven by jealousy to inform on the two Sicilians, thereby violating his own code of honor and ethics. Too proud and stubborn to acknowledge that he was wrong, Eddie challenges the elder immigrant, Marco, to a fight, in which Eddie is killed.

Eddie's attorney, Alfieri, serves as a narrator-chorus in this play, reminiscent of the chorus in Greek tragedy. The play's basic theme is concerned with ethical choice and principle, themes that Miller explored in his earlier plays. The theme is particularly poignant here, as Miller wrote this play while in the midst of his difficulties with the House Un-American Activities Committee. His mind was much on questions of ethics and values.

Eddie's depiction is more psychosexual than that of most Miller characters. He sometimes displays remarkable, barely controllable passion. During such lapses, the audience glimpses the deep-seated incestuousness and deeply repressed homosexual tendencies of his nature.

Miller uses the attorney Alfieri as the dramatic device through whom the audience gains a perspective on Eddie. Alfieri cannot offer a rational explanation for Eddie's actions, but he can, from his detached point of view, relate them to Eddie's roots. In the end, Alfieri says, "I think I will love him more than all my sensible clients," revealing the extent to which Eddie has affected him.

Eddie's act of betrayal is motivated by strong, deep, inner forces that he can neither understand nor control. These forces dishonor his own self-image, and he loses his identity and his reason for being. Death is his only out, as it has been for the protagonists in many Miller dramas.

Resources

The University of Michigan and the University of Texas at Austin have major Arthur Miller collections. The Theater Collection in the New York City Public Library has holdings of Miller papers, including files of his newspaper and magazine articles and the typescript of "They Too Arise." Its unpublished revision, "The Grass Still Grows," is in the Academic Center Library of the University of Texas at Austin, as are the typescripts of Miller's unpublished screenplay "The Hook" and his unpublished short story, "In Memorium" [sic], the basis for *Death of a Salesman*. The typescripts of *No Villain* and *Honors at Dawn* are in the Hopwood Room of the University of Michigan, which also has files of the student newspaper, *Michigan Daily*, to which Miller contributed. The Library of Congress holds the typescript of

Miller's unpublished radio play "The Four Freedoms." Other sources of information for students of Arthur Miller include the following:

The Arthur Miller Society. This organization promotes the study of Miller and his work through conferences, panels, and calls for papers. The society also publishes a newspaper, *The X*. The society's official Web site has membership information, as well as listings of current Miller events, biography and bibliography of Miller's life and works, and links to related sites. (http://www.metalab.unc.edu/miller/)

American Drama **6.1: Arthur Miller Issue.** The fall 1996 issue of the journal *American Drama* was devoted entirely to the study of Arthur Miller. This version accessible on line contains abstracts of the printed articles as well as the full text of two interviews from previous issues. (http://blues.fd1.uc.edu/www/amdrama/61miller.html)

Arthur Miller's *Death of a Salesman*. This Web site was created for the 1999 revival of the play at the Eugene O'Neill Theater in New York City. It features information about the cast and crew of this production, as well as reviews of important past productions, information about Miller and his work, and even a study guide to the play. (http://www.deathofasalesman.com/)

R. BAIRD SHUMAN

Marianne Moore

BORN: November 15, 1887, Kirkwood, Missouri
DIED: February 5, 1972, New York, New York
IDENTIFICATION: Early to mid-twentieth-century poet and literary critic who promoted the work of major twentieth-century modernist poets, becoming an important and respected voice in the literary movement of her time.

Marianne Moore's interests ranged widely, and her knowledge of literary history and the sciences was extensive. In her essays and reviews she wrote of animals, French and German authors, music, artists and painting, ballet, drama, film, sculpture, and baseball and its players. Her main interest was contemporary poetry and poets. She referred to her own verse as poetry for lack of any other category in which to put it, but others considered it exceptional in its use of rhythm and vivid detail. She favored natural rhythms and concealed rhyme. In all writing, she strove for compression, simplicity, and precision.

The Writer's Life

On November 15, 1887, Marianne Moore was born in Kirkwood, Missouri, a suburb of St. Louis, the second child of Mary and John Milton Moore. Her brother John was seventeen months older than she. When Moore was still a small child, her father, an engineer, failed in business and suffered a nervous breakdown. He went to live with his parents in Ohio and never returned. Mary and the two children went to live with Mary's father, John Riddle Warner, pastor of the First Presbyterian Church in Kirkwood.

Childhood. In 1894, when Reverend Warner died, Mary Moore moved with her children to Carlisle, Pennsylvania, where she had relatives. Despite these early misfortunes, Moore had a happy childhood, enjoying close and affectionate family relations, pets—puppies, kittens, even an alligator—joyous holiday gatherings, and outings with friends. In Carlisle, she attended high school, where she developed an enduring interest in art and drawing. She studied Latin and German—which she found difficult—and biology. Her mother especially would continue to play an important part in Moore's life, providing criticism of her writing and instilling a respect for clear, simple expression.

College Years. In 1905 Moore entered Bryn Mawr, where she continued to have difficulty with languages, at first failing, but eventually passing, both German and Italian. At college she became independent and self-reliant, despite her timidity and homesickness. She read and admired the prose style of seventeenth-century authors and began writing her own poetry. By 1909, she had published thirteen poems and worked on the campus literary magazine. At Bryn Mawr she made the acquaintance of Hilda Doolittle, later known as the poet H. D., who would eventually publish some of Moore's poetry and introduce Moore to Ezra Pound and William Carlos Williams and the literary circle surrounding these two major American poets. Both Pound and Williams would become important to Moore in later years.

Fledgling Poet. Moore graduated from Bryn Mawr in 1909 and returned to Carlisle, where she remained for several years teaching commercial law, typing, and related subjects at the United States Industrial Indian School. In 1911 she and her mother traveled

Moore on her graduation day at Bryn Mawr in 1909. The quirky, independent thinker had already made strides in her literary career.

to Europe, touring England and the museums of Paris. Meanwhile, Moore continued writing poetry, and in 1915, one of her poems was published in the British journal *Egoist*. She published several more in American journals, such as *Poetry*. Ezra Pound praised her poetry and considered her an important member of the new modernist poetic movement. By 1918, Moore was also receiving encouragement from such important poets as William Carlos Williams and T. S. Eliot.

When Moore's brother, John, who had become a Presbyterian minister, was appointed pastor of a church in Chatham, New Jersey, in 1916, Moore and her mother moved there and took charge of the household. Moore began frequent visits to New York City, mingling with members of the literary world. She continued writing and publishing poetry. When John joined the Navy as a chaplain in 1918, Moore and her mother moved to an apartment in Greenwich Village. There Moore tutored, taught in a private girls' school, and worked part-time in a branch of the New York Public Library.

Growing Stature. Friends published several of Moore's poems in England in 1921 without her knowledge. Another collection, *Observations*, was published by her friends in America in 1924. This volume won her an award from *The Dial* in the same year, which included two thousand dollars. As the country's most prestigious literary periodical, *The Dial* brought Moore increased respect, and in 1925 she became its editor. Although the position allowed her no time for her own poetry, she was able to hone her ideas on literary theory and was introduced to diverse points of view and a wide range of subjects. Moore continued editing the journal until its last issue in 1929.

Full Maturity. When *The Dial* ceased publication, Moore returned to writing poetry. She had moved with her mother the previous years from Greenwich Village to another apartment in Brooklyn, where she would remain until shortly before her death. *Selected Poems* appeared in

When Moore was awarded the Pulitzer Prize, it served as a sort of lifetime achievement award in recognition of her profound, textured, and consistently original lyrics. Moore is seen here shortly after winning the prize in 1952.

1935, with an introduction by T. S. Eliot, and won the Ernest Harstock Memorial Prize. A year later, *The Pangolin and Other Verse* was published in England. Moore published *What Are Years* in the United States in 1941. During this time, she taught composition in Massachusetts and began lecturing at poetry seminars at Harvard, Vassar, and the University of California.

Throughout the 1940s Moore won many awards and fellowships, including the Shelley Memorial Award from the Poetry Society of America (1940), the Harriet Monroe Prize for Poetry (1944), the Contemporary Poetry Patrons Prize (1944), a Guggenheim Fellowship (1945), and a joint grant from the National Institute of Arts and Letters and the American Academy of Arts and Letters (1946). In 1946 she began translating Jean de La Fontaine's *Fables choisies, mises en vers* (1668–1694).

While this work was just beginning, Moore's mother died, leaving a vacuum in Moore's life

Dragons, the central motif in this mural from Indonesia's Court of Justice, figure in Moore's ninth book of poems, *O to Be a Dragon*. The collection reflects the playful quality of her work as well as the subtle influence of La Fontaine's fables.

that she filled with continued writing and translating. In 1947 she was elected a member of the National Institute of Arts and Letters, and she received several honorary degrees. In 1951 she published *Collected Poems*, which was followed by a trio of important awards: the National Book Award, the Pulitzer Prize for poetry, and the Bollingen Prize in Poetry, all in 1952.

Three years later, her translation *Selected Fables of La Fontaine* (1955) was published. In the same year a collection of her essays and reviews appeared under the title *Predilections*. During this time the Ford Motor Company sought Moore's advice on a name for its new car. Moore returned several suggestions, none of which were adopted—Ford ultimately chose Edsel—but the correspondence between the two parties was published in *The New Yorker*.

Last Years. Moore's later years were devoted to writing poetry and producing books of poems and prose. A small volume of Moore's poems, *Like a Bulwark*, was published in 1956, and *O to Be a Dragon* followed in 1959. *A Marianne Moore Reader*, published in 1961, brings together several poems, some translations of La Fontaine's fables, some essays from *Predilections*, the Ford letters, and an interview. Moore followed this work the next year with a dramatization of the 1812 novel *The Absentee* by Maria Edgeworth.

Tell Me, Tell Me came out in 1966. All of this activity culminated in 1967 in the publication of *The Complete Poems of Marianne Moore*, after which Moore continued to contribute small prose pieces to popular magazines. Moore died on February 5, 1972, in New York. Fourteen years later, her writing found its final expression with the publication of *The Complete Prose of Marianne Moore* (1986).

HIGHLIGHTS IN MOORE'S LIFE

1887   Marianne Moore is born on November 15, in Kirkwood, Missouri.
1894   Goes with mother and brother to live with relatives in Carlisle, Pennsylvania.
1905   Enters Bryn Mawr College; begins writing poetry.
1909   Earns bachelor's degree from Bryn Mawr; returns to Carlisle, where she teaches at United States Industrial Indian School.
1915   Publishes poems in *The Egoist* and *Poetry*.
1916   Moves with her mother to Chatham, New Jersey, to keep house for her brother.
1918   Moves to Greenwich Village with her mother; tutors and does secretarial work in a private girls' school.
1921   Moore's first book of poems is published by friends in England.
1924   *Observations* is published; Moore receives a two-thousand-dollar award from *The Dial*.
1925   Moore becomes editor of *The Dial*.
1929   Resumes writing poetry after *The Dial* ceases publication.
1935   Publishes *Selected Poems*.
1940   Wins the Shelley Memorial Award.
1941   Publishes *What Are Years*.
1944   Wins Harriet Monroe Prize for Poetry and the Contemporary Poetry Patrons Prize.
1945   Is awarded a Guggenheim Fellowship.
1946   Receives a joint grant from the National Institute of Arts and Letters and the American Academy of Arts and Letters; begins translating Jean de La Fontaine's *Fables*.
1947   Mother dies; Moore is elected to the National Institute of Arts and Letters.
1951   Publishes *Collected Poems*.
1952   Receives the National Book Award, the Pulitzer Prize for poetry, and the Bollingen Prize.
1955   Publishes *Selected Fables of La Fontaine*.
1961   Publishes *A Marianne Moore Reader*.
1962   Publishes *The Absentee*, a dramatization of a novel by Maria Edgeworth.
1967   *The Complete Poems of Marianne Moore* is published.
1972   Dies on February 5, in New York City.

The Writer's Work

Marianne Moore is best known for her poetry, although her prose is also widely admired. It could be argued that she was so consistent in all her writing that everything she wrote was a poem. In her prose and poetry alike, one finds precise expression, a restrained excitement for her subjects, compression, concrete details, and rhythmic elegance.

Issues in Moore's Writing. From the beginning of her writing career, Moore dedicated herself to sincerity of expression and precision in the use of language. She valued these qualities in the works of others. Ezra Pound and William Carlos Williams were among the first to admire her poetry for its natural rhythms, attention to particulars, and concrete images. Her talent for writing poetry in open form was ideally suited to this new generation of writers. Her ability to focus on particulars yet suggest a wide array of impressions and associations gave her a distinctive style, and the respect her writing generated made her an important voice in poetry for almost half a century.

Moore's poetry demonstrates the principles that she discussed in her prose: precise language, clarity of image, compression, natural rhythm, the unaccented line, and the hidden rhyme or the light rhyme. Although she believed that enthusiasm was important in expression, she cultivated restraint and praised the writers whose work demonstrated these same qualities. She disliked anything artificial or insincere and disapproved of coarse subjects or language, criticizing its use by others.

Themes in Moore's Writing. As an editor and reviewer, Moore promoted the literary principles she most admired, praising the work of those who exemplified them. In an early review, she praises the poetry of E. E. Cummings for its visual variety and rhythms, qualities found in her own poetry. In another review, she compliments poet Wallace Stevens's "sharp, solemn, rhapsodic elegant pieces of eloquence." She remarks of the ballplayer, Casey Stengel, that he was "a master of restraint and elegant comportment." Motion was especially important to Moore, whether in the rhythms of poetry, in the way a baseball player catches a ball, or in the way a ballerina dances. Virtually everything that caught her eye expressed some meaning beyond itself, just

By the 1960s Moore was a minor celebrity and one of the *grandes dames* of American letters. The designer Stutley created this black velvet tricornered hat for her, which became one of her signatures.

1038

as objects in her poetry seem to have both a physical and an abstract quality.

Subjects in Moore's Writing. In her writing and in her private life, Moore was remarkable for her discriminating judgment, and the range of her interests surprised even her friends. One would expect her to appreciate writers and literary subjects, but she also liked motor cars and baseball players, and she wrote of both. She reviewed only the books that she liked, and her appreciation included sports, animals, poetry, ballet, novels, art, and music. She discussed literary theory, philosophy, landscaping, history, biography, travel, and style with the same ease and clarity with which she discussed arachnids, flowers, and birds.

Moore's favorite subjects, however, were writers and writing, and she wrote many essays on the principles of good writing. All these subjects find their way into her poetry, but in different ways. Many of her poems are like essays, defining the essence of her subject—be it an octopus, marriage, propriety, or poetry itself. She told people that the subjects of her poetry came unexpectedly and almost compelled her to write of them. Her poems were in an important sense discoveries for her, opportunities to give life to what had come to her as an impression, a feeling, a thought.

Moore's Literary Legacy. Although Moore is best known for her poetry, which brought her many major awards, her essays and reviews are also an important part of her literary legacy. In her years as editor of *The Dial*, she brought to public attention the work of such female writers as Louise Bogan and Hilda Doolittle (the poet H. D.), and many of her reviews were devoted to emerging poets such as Wallace Stevens, William Carlos Williams, T. S. Eliot, and others. She wrote frequently of Henry James and devoted essays to him and to Sir Francis Bacon.

Moore leans on the rail of the crowded Yankee Stadium in New York after throwing out the first ball of the 1968 season. Known for her wide-ranging tastes, it was no secret that the somewhat reserved poet was also an ardent fan of the sport.

SOME INSPIRATIONS BEHIND MOORE'S WORK

Marianne Moore admired the poetry of Ezra Pound, T. S. Eliot, E. E. Cummings, and William Carlos Williams, feeling an affinity for its new rhythms and inspired by its experiments in rhyme. She joined this circle of modernist poets, turning from traditional forms, including rhyme, meter, and stanzaic patterns. The new poetry did contain rhyme, rhythm, and stanzas, but the emphasis was on natural form, one that reflected the poet's immediate sense and the poem's subject. Moore's literary friends welcomed new ideas about literature, had wide interests, and were passionate about poetry. Artistic innovation was prized, and the group's chief enemies were mediocrity, insincerity, and a devotion to materialism and stodgy literary traditions. The new generation of poets sought a language free of sentimentality and artificiality. Moore's own principles meshed fully with these views.

Although spirituality is a strong element in Moore's poetry, so is concrete detail. Moore sought to discover and express a connection between the object and its spiritual value. She admired people of high moral character, especially women, such as Isak Dinesen and ballerina Anna Pavlova, whose accomplishments derived from an independent mind and spirit.

Moore had a lifelong high regard for Henry James, admiring his attention to the particular and his affection for fantasy. In one of her major essays, "Henry James as a Characteristic American," she highlights some of the qualities that inspired her: his idealism and his belief that the "aura is more than the thing." Perhaps no better summary of Moore's own poetry can be found.

Moore demonstrated through her poems that one could write poetry of the highest quality on a great variety of subjects, including the wild mouse, the swan, the buffalo, or the candelabrum-tree. However, it is what Moore does with these animal and vegetable kingdoms that elevates her writing above the ordinary and gives it lasting value. She imbues her particular subject with rhythmic life and visual clarity. Her powers of expression and observation transform an object into a presence that one can scarcely forget.

BIBLIOGRAPHY

Bloom, Harold. *Marianne Moore*. New York: Chelsea House, 1987.

Costello, Bonnie, Celeste Goodridge, and Cristanne Miller. *The Selected Letters of Marianne Moore*. New York: Knopf, 1997.

Engel, Bernard F. *Marianne Moore*. New York: Twayne Publishers, 1964.

Erickson, Darlene Williams. *Illusion Is More Precise than Precision: The Poetry of Marianne Moore*. Tuscaloosa: University of Alabama Press, 1992.

Hall, Donald. *Marianne Moore: The Cage and the Animal*. New York: Pegasus, 1970.

Holley, Margaret. *The Poetry of Marianne Moore: A Study in Voice and Value*. New York: Cambridge University Press, 1987.

Miller, Cristanne. *Marianne Moore: Questions of Authority*. Cambridge, Mass.: Harvard University Press, 1995.

Molesworth, Charles. *Marianne Moore: A Literary Life*. Boston: Northeastern University Press, 1991.

Parisi, Joseph. *Marianne Moore: The Art of a Modernist*. Ann Arbor, Mich.: UMI Research Press, 1990.

Willis, Patricia C., ed. *Marianne Moore: Woman and Poet*. Orono, Maine: National Poetry Foundation, 1990.

Reader's Guide to Major Works

THE COMPLETE POEMS OF MARIANNE MOORE

Genre: Poetry
Subgenre: Open Forms
Published: New York, 1967
Time period: Timeless present
Setting: Various

Themes and Issues. Marianne Moore's final collection of poems contains 120 poems arranged chronologically. A quick survey of their titles shows that her interests remained consistent throughout her career. She wrote often about animals and vegetables, seeking to define their individuality and their essential nature. She was always attracted to the unusual, and many of her animals, such as the pangolin, the jerboa, and the paper nautilus, are unusual. However, she also wrote of the commonplace monkey, the snail, the goat, frogs, and jellyfish.

Even in those poems that deal with machines and other inanimate subjects, Moore sought to define the object as though it had a spirit that was both worthy of notice and tantalizingly elusive as well as to express its significance. She probed beneath appearances often in a very indirect manner. This way of writing, layering one subject upon others, makes her poems highly individual, complex, and intriguing.

One of the fundamental themes in Moore's poetry is the search to understand the relation of imagination—or the mind in general—to the world outside itself. This search led Moore in many poems to a focus on definition. In perhaps her most famous poem, "Poetry," she combines her quest for understanding and definition, saying that true poets are "'literalists of / the imagination'—above / insolence and triviality. . . ." Poetry, she adds, consists of "'imaginary gardens with real toads in them.'" Here is expressed Moore's poetic credo, her aim: to render in descriptive detail and concrete image the poet's vision. Poetry must capture what is significant and somehow convey that significance to the reader. Moore's poetry is in many ways a search for significance in the things that captured her attention.

The variety of Moore's interests gained her a reputation for being somewhat eccentric and unpredictable. She surprised many people by admiring baseball players, for instance, and for writing about unusual creatures and objects, from the jerboa to the icosahedron. Yet her interests included the most commonplace ob-

Like Moore's poem on the subject, a paper nautilus is intricate and detailed, multichambered and ever increasing in complexity and concision.

jects, as she demonstrates in a poem titled "A Face," seeking its essential meaning. Because Moore delivers the surface features of her subject with remarkable detail, some readers miss the deeper significance of her poetry. Early in her career, T. S. Eliot thought it necessary to defend her poetry against the charge that it lacked emotion, arguing that a careful reading would uncover it. Much of the emotional energy in Moore's poetry is directed toward rendering the imaginary gardens and real toads, making of them a significant union. Her emotion is evident in her inspired effort to capture the essential character of things.

The Poems. The issue of emotion becomes central to Moore's poetry, both for the reader and for the poet herself. Some readers see the poem's descriptive detail and imagery as a kind of barrier between Moore and her subject. One of Moore's literary precepts was that the writer should show restraint, and in her own endeavor to achieve it and to remain above the trivial and overly personal, she focused on description, on characterizing her subject. In that way, she directed attention away from her own feelings. A poem's intensity is evident in its skillful definition and description, and the poet's emotional attachment to her subject is confused with how she gives life to that subject. The issue for the reader, then, is how the emotional content of the poem is expressed—how, that is, it invests the poem.

One of the clues to a poem's emotional content is its length. "Marriage," one of Moore's longest poems, runs a little over eight full-length pages and ranges from the modern-day practice of exchanging vows at the altar to Adam and Eve, from this world of public display to a world of incandescent stars and fruit. It includes images of gold, snakeskin, raw silk, "a crouching mythological monster," emerald mines, opuntias, and more.

The poem is based on the biblical Garden of Eden, which symbolizes for Moore not only the beginning of marriage but also the fertile setting in which marital love takes place. In this sense, love becomes entwined with the elements of the garden, exotic flowers, and nature's general outgrowth. At the same time, Moore ranges through a wide landscape: from Heaven and Eden to the modern world, the animal kingdom, and elsewhere. Her travels reflect the nature of love and marriage: It is as variegated as nature, as sinuous as a snake (and

Poems such as "A Face" reveal the deceptive power of Moore's descriptive bravura. The fine delineation of surface becomes in the end a form of poetic inversion, a token of unspoken complexities and inner depths.

as dangerous), as complicated and as rich as love and marriage. The poem comes to symbolize what it seeks to define.

Readers both revel in and complain of the difficulty of following Moore's mind as it works on her subject. Some say that her poetry defies analysis, and they are sometimes stymied by the lack of linearity in some of her poems. In "An Octopus," for example, Moore offers a definition that takes the reader through myriad transformations and worlds. She dislodges the reader's complacent expectations by making her octopus "of ice" and placing the creature "beneath a sea of shifting snow-dunes." The creature bears "dots of cyclamen-red and maroon" and has "pseudo-podia / made of glass that will bend. . . ." In this way, the poem takes on the physical qualities of the octopus, sinuous, mysterious, rare, and exotic. The icy chill it inspires reflects its own form. As she herself once said, "Form is synonymous with content—must be. . . ."

Analysis. All her poems together represent a record of Moore's search to understand the nature of the world, which includes the animal and vegetable kingdoms as well as the human world. The record turns out to be a map of her own imagination, and in that sense it helps to explain the fascination her poetry has inspired. The more she describes the worlds she envisions, the more elusive she becomes, and the more fascinating.

Poets admire her use of light rhymes, rhythms, and descriptive powers to create poems that seem to take on the shapes of her subjects. She said poetry "is not a thing of tunes, but of heightened consciousness. . . ." The heightened consciousness combines rhythm, emotion, and image into something that exists beyond a simple combination of these elements. Each takes on a life of its own; each poem is both a statement and a picture of Moore's subject. Because each poem is a definition of the poet's vision, each becomes an aspect of the poet. All together, they define Moore herself.

SOURCES FOR FURTHER STUDY

Allen, Mary. "Controlled Creatures: Marianne Moore." In *Animals in American Literature*, edited by Mary Allen. Urbana: University of Illinois Press, 1983.

Carrington, Ruth. "Marianne Moore's Metaphysical Giraffe." In *Marianne Moore: Woman and Poet*, edited by Patricia Willis. Orono, Maine: National Poetry Foundation, 1990.

Gregory, Elizabeth. "'Silence' and Restraint." In *Marianne Moore: Woman and Poet*, edited by Patricia Willis. Orono, Maine: National Poetry Foundation, 1990.

POETRY

- 1921 Poems
- 1924 Observations
- 1935 Selected Poems
- 1936 The Pangolin and Other Verse
- 1941 What Are Years
- 1944 Nevertheless
- 1951 Collected Poems
- 1956 Like a Bulwark
- 1959 O to Be a Dragon
- 1966 Tell Me, Tell Me
- 1967 The Complete Poems of Marianne Moore (reissued with minor changes in 1981)

PLAY

- 1962 The Absentee (adapted from Maria Edgeworth's novel)

NONFICTION

- 1955 Predilections

MISCELLANEOUS

- 1961 A Marianne Moore Reader
- 1986 The Complete Prose of Marianne Moore

TRANSLATION

- 1955 Selected Fables of La Fontaine

THE COMPLETE PROSE OF MARIANNE MOORE

Genre: Nonfiction
Subgenre: Essays and reviews
Published: New York, 1986
Time period: 1910s to 1960s
Setting: United States

Themes and Issues. This collection, arranged chronologically, contains three-fourths of all Moore's published prose, from 1907 to the late 1960s. It includes almost three hundred essays and reviews, ten short stories, and an appendix that contains many miscellaneous writings: brief, pointed comments used on the dust jackets of other people's books; questionnaires to which she responded; a list of her favorite books; and comments about herself and the principles by which she lived and wrote.

Two-thirds of the nearly two hundred major essays, ranging in length from a couple of pages to more than twelve, address literary topics, principally poets and their works. The range of these essays shows that, from her years at *The Dial* onward, Moore promoted the work of artists, both famous and little known, who in her judgment offered something of value. She rarely gave a negative opinion of a work and

Moore was in no way a specialist, focusing only on her poetry to the exclusion of other things. Widely read and interested in a diverse range of subjects, she embraced all the arts and championed young practitioners everywhere. In Moses Soyer's 1938 painting *WPA Artists*, novices perfect their craft.

preferred to let the work speak for itself by quoting extensively from it. She especially favored the major poets of her day, T. S. Eliot, Wallace Stevens, E. E. Cummings, William Butler Yeats, and Ezra Pound. The longest essay in the book, in fact, discusses the poetry of W. H. Auden. She also championed female writers, including Virginia Woolf, Harriet Monroe, Edith Sitwell, Emily Dickinson, and many others.

The Essays. Generally, Moore liked the exceptional and the excellent, wherever she found it, in books and in the world, and she scrutinized both with an intense curiosity and a deep appetite. These collected writings show the qualities of mind for which she was famous and admired: enthusiasm for her subjects; precise language and extensive use of quotations; a keen eye for the significant detail; and a wide, often exotic, vocabulary that befits her varied interests. In her prose, she sought to capture the spirit and importance of her subject and to express her appreciation of it rather than to simply expose its flaws and shortcomings. In this way, her reviews are very personal, even idiosyncratic, but her comments were admired by the best writers of her day.

She both praised and practiced exactness in stating ideas, and she frequently promoted, by example and by precept, the fundamentals of good writing. Instinctively drawn to writing that was simply constructed and concentrated in meaning, she confessed to having a "mania for straight writing." She did not like connectives in sentences and, like the poet Ezra Pound, preferred the subject-verb-object arrangement. For her, effective writing is infused with passion, and she agreed with William Faulkner that the ultimate aim of writing should be to lift one's heart. She believed that clarity depends on precision, both in descriptive detail and in one's choice of words, and if her sentences are crowded, the language is nevertheless pointed and exact.

In Moore's mind, nothing was simply itself; everything connected to something else and in that way took on added meaning. She felt that "'The fabric of existence weaves itself whole. . . ,'" quoting composer Charles Ives. Consequently, she was as much at home discussing maps, snakes, baseball, painting, the circus, and fashion as she was writing literary criticism and reviewing new poetry. Her prose constantly looks outward both in its subject matter and in its metaphorical connections. In a long essay about her own neighborhood, Brooklyn, she rarely mentions herself. Trees, people, buildings, schools, all form part of her reminiscence; all contribute to what Brooklyn meant to her. The reader looks through Moore's

Unpretentious and always democratic and generous in her praise, Moore extolled the qualities that both an accomplished athlete and gifted writer share—talent, discipline, commitment, and endurance. In Jacob Lawrence's 1949 *Strike*, physical prowess is put to the test.

eyes and sees better from that perspective.

Another long essay, "The Knife," begins with a description of one of Moore's favorite knives and takes the reader on a long journey to Greece and Italy, mentioning architecture, shields, and seafaring, and ending on one of her favorite sayings of Confucius, "'If there be a knife of resentment in the heart, the mind fails to act with precision.'" The knife's symbolic value coexists with its physical nature, and each gives value to the other.

One of Moore's passions was baseball, in particular baseball players. She saw in them "miracles of dexterity," admiring how one moved or another made a difficult catch. She praises the fortitude, stamina, and courage of the Cardinals' manager in his struggle to overcome tuberculosis and praises another player for struggling through his physical disabilities. She felt that the way these athletes dealt with their private struggles typifies the spirit of those who play the game. Their dedication to excellence, combined with their physical grace, inspired Moore, and she shared her feelings so that others might be inspired as well.

Analysis. In her later years, Moore contributed essays to popular magazines such as *Vogue*, *The Atlantic Monthly*, and others. Her style of writing won her a new audience, and she continued to be admired for her eclectic taste and point of view as well as for her precision, complexity, and subtlety of expression. Her knowledge of history, science, art, and many other subjects was vast and detailed. She was the epitome of taste, intelligence, good judgment, and literary integrity.

Without being stubborn or narrow-minded, she adhered firmly to her principles and to her very personal style of writing. Her ability to create word pictures of surprising vividness and variety depended to a great extent on her powers of observation and eye for detail. Her dexterity with language was a reflection of the dexterity of her mind, and the liveliness of her observations was an extension of her passion and enthusiasm for discovery and expression.

SOURCES FOR FURTHER STUDY

Borroff, Marie. "Marianne Moore's Promotional Prose." In *Marianne Moore*, edited by Harold Bloom. New York: Chelsea House, 1987.

Costello, Bonnie. "Strong Enchantments." *The New Republic* 195, no. 26 (December 19, 1986): 30–34.

Plimpton, George, ed. *Women Writers at Work: "The Paris Review" Interviews*. New York: Modern Library, 1998.

Other Works

"GRANITE AND STEEL" (1966). Marianne Moore often saw significance in machinery and in other things fabricated by human ingenuity. The subject of this poem, the Brooklyn Bridge, symbolized for her the connection between human aspiration and inanimate nature. It also signified the confluence of nationalities, for the bridge resulted from "French perspicacity" and German tenacity. Most important of all, however, is the bridge's function—to span, to connect, to bring together. It is "an actuality," she says at the poem's end, a manifest emblem, as her poems are, of the human mind's ability to discover, and to create, unity.

"THE MOUSE METAMORPHOSED INTO A MAID" (1954). Although this poem is a translation of one of La Fontaine's fables, Moore's characteristic manner makes it her own. She opens with an arresting image and a somewhat ironic comment: "A mouse fell from a screech-owl's beak—a thing that I can not pretend / To be Hindoo enough to have cared / To pick up." From this intriguing start, the poem builds an ironic argument, namely, that not even black magic can transform a mouse into a girl. All along, this statement is opposed by the poem's form, which demonstrates that art can unite the mouse and the girl—or anything, for that matter—by bringing them together in a poem and illuminating their essential unity.

The poem shows also how Moore can turn prosaic lines into poetry by placing them in a poetic context that connects the lines to the major themes of the poem, thereby infusing them with the tone and intensity of the poem's quest for understanding and expression. One stanza begins thus: "We retain the traits of the place from which we came. This tale / Bears me out. . . ." Except for the line break, this could be from one of her essays, yet it forms a link in the poetic development of her theme, which concludes with the idea that the nature of every creature is unchanging. The erudite discussion contributes to the total picture of a world in which strange combinations form a single, unifying spirit. The lines of prose give a flavor of the ordinary world, even as they are transformed into poetry by the surprising combinations.

"TELL ME, TELL ME" (1966). This later poem typifies how Moore's mind worked over a subject and brought together quotations, lines of prose, and obscure allusions to make them all one. The poem demonstrates how central to her art is her use of seemingly unrelated and unpoetic elements. The rhyme scheme of the five stanzas is intricate: The first two lines of each stanza rhyme with the fifth line, and the sixth and ninth lines rhyme. Occasionally, too, internal rhymes occur.

The first stanza establishes the poem's central idea: The poet seeks to escape from her own "egocentricity," which blinds her to the continuity of all things. The next two stanzas illustrate the "geometry of a fantasy" that exists in the poet's mind, which jumbles together an image of "Lord Nelson's revolving diamond rosette," some mice, a quotation from Chinese literature, a remembrance of Beatrix Potter, whose story *The Tailor of Gloucester* appeared in 1902, and other elements. A quotation from the autobiography of the novelist Henry James expresses her dilemma: In his education, he "'breathed inconsistency and drank / contradiction. . . .'" She wishes to escape the "viper's traffic-knot" that has made her a "refugee from verbal ferocity. . . ."

In the end, both the poet and the reader are rescued by the poem itself. By submitting to her mental jumble and writing a poem about it, she finds—or creates—an end to her "captivity." The power to weave together all these elements into a single statement delivers her from their thrall. Paradoxically, in submitting to the disarray, she escapes it, and the mediat-

An animal lover, the various members of the natural world continually found their way into Moore's poems. Here a large bird perches on her arm at the Brooklyn Zoo in 1953.

ing power is art, which directs attention from egocentricity to universality.

"TO A SNAIL" (1935). In this poem of only twelve lines, Moore displays the kind of virtuosity and erudition that characterize many of her poems, using quotations to develop her poetic statement. The poem's central metaphor equates the snail with writing style and, at the same time, writing style with the snail. This combination would produce only a witty and surprising association were it not for the poem's serious point, that two subjects as different as a snail and good writing are part of a unified whole that this poem comes to symbolize, for in it nature and art entwine.

The poem's abstract language—laden with words such as "compression," "contractility," "concomitant," and "phenomenon"—lends an ironic contrast to its ostensible subject, the very earthy and commonplace snail. Moore was a master in creating a poetic image of the continuity that exists among the wide variety of subjects that her questing and inquisitive mind encountered.

Resources

St. Lawrence University in Canton, New York, has the Marianne Moore Collection, an archive of photos, correspondence, and poems and articles by and about Moore. Other sources of interest to students of Moore include the following:

Academy of American Poets, Poetry Exhibits, Marianne Moore. The Academy of American Poets has an informative Web site with a discussion on Moore's relationship to the modernist movement in poetry, a selected bibliography of her work, texts of several poems, and links to other Moore sites. (http://www.poets.org/poets/poets.cfm?prmlD=97)

Audio Recordings. Moore is recorded reading "Bird-Witted" on an audiocassette entitled *A Century of Recorded Poetry* and released by Rhino/Word Beat in 1996. Of equal interest is Caedmon's *Marianne Moore Reading Her Poetry* (1972), which includes Moore reading the fables of La Fontaine. Some of Moore's work has also been sung. William Sharp recorded two Moore works in 1988 for New World Records. The Wellesley College Choir also recorded "O to Be a Dragon," "A Jelly-Fish," "To a Chameleon," and "To Victor Hugo of My Crow Pluto," released by Rhino Records in 1996.

Spotlight on Voices and Visions, Marianne Moore. This Web site accompanying the Annenberg/CPB video series on poetry, *Voices and Visions* contains useful biographical and critical information and links, as well as a video recording of Moore's poem "The Fish." (http://www.learner.org/catalog/literature/vvseries/vvspot/moore.html)

Video Recordings. The Canadian Learning Company released *Marianne Moore in Her Own Image* (1988), an audiovisual that includes reminiscences about Moore, selections from her poetry illustrated with visuals, insights into her life, and interviews with the poet. In *Marianne Moore*, produced by the New York Center for Visual History in 1995, Moore's life and career are reviewed through photographs and film clips. She is also shown reading her poetry, and other writers and literary critics offer critical and anecdotal commentary.

BERNARD E. MORRIS

Toni Morrison

BORN: February 18, 1931, Lorain, Ohio
IDENTIFICATION: Late twentieth-century African American writer best known for her novels depicting the struggles of African American women in a white, male-dominated culture.

Toni Morrison published her first novel in 1970, at the peak of the Civil Rights movement and at the beginning of the women's movement. Both African Americans and feminists have claimed her books as significant depictions of their struggles. *Beloved* (1987), her most important work to date, won the Pulitzer Prize for fiction in 1988. Morrison was awarded the Nobel Prize in Literature in 1993, making her the first African American woman to achieve this honor. Her books have been enormously popular, critically acclaimed, and frequently taught in college and high school classrooms. With a number of novels to her credit, as well as a play and a book of literary criticism, Morrison is one of the most important figures in late twentieth-century American literature.

The Writer's Life

Toni Morrison was born Chloe Anthony Wofford on February 18, 1931, in Lorain, Ohio, a steel-mill town on Lake Erie twenty-five miles from Cleveland. She was the second of George and Ramah Willis Wofford's four children.

George Wofford held three jobs simultaneously for years, supporting the family through the Great Depression of the 1930s. He had strong views about race, believing that white people were genetically incapable of overcoming their prejudice against blacks and trusting no white person. Morrison's mother, on the other hand, believed that race relations could be improved through education.

Childhood. Morrison's family lived in a neighborhood populated by both blacks and whites, including many European immigrants. When Morrison was two years old, her parents were late paying the rent, and the landlord tried to burn the house down with the family inside—a story Morrison heard repeatedly while growing up. Morrison was the only African American child in her first-grade class and the only student who could read at the beginning of school. She dreamed of being a ballerina like Maria Tallchief.

Morrison began working at age twelve, learning from an early age to balance many responsibilities. In high school she was an excellent student and participated in extracurricular activities, including the student council, the National Honor Society, and school yearbook editorial staff.

The Future Writer. The Wofford family enjoyed storytelling, and Morrison learned much African American folklore from her relatives. Her father told thrilling ghost stories, and Morrison's grandparents, who lived with the family, told stories about their childhoods in the South, where Morrison's grandfather had been freed from slavery at age five. The family stories ignited Morrison's

The figure in Robert Henri's 1907 painting *Eva Green* (Wichita Art Museum, Wichita, Kansas) bears the features both of an adult and a little girl. Precocious and fiercely intelligent, as a child Morrison always seemed to stand out from her peers.

imagination and her interest in history. Her extensive reading included the works of Fyodor Dostoyevski, Gustave Flaubert, Jane Austen, Ernest Hemingway, Willa Cather, and William Faulkner.

College Years. In 1949 Morrison enrolled at Howard University, a prestigious black college in Washington, D.C. It was there that she began using the nickname Toni, from her middle name, Anthony. At that time, very little African American literature was assigned, and she majored in English and minored in classics. One of her most memorable activities was performing with the Howard University Players, a well-respected acting troupe. With the Players, she toured the Deep South for the first time.

After graduating from Howard in 1953, Morrison earned a master's degree in English at Cornell University. There she wrote a thesis on suicide in the novels of William Faulkner and Virginia Woolf, completed in 1955.

The publication of *Song of Solomon* confirmed Morrison's presence as one of the most original and important novelists of her generation. This still is taken from the PBS program *The Originals: The Writer in America*, which featured Morrison as part of its seventh installment in 1978.

Early Career. After earning her master's degree from Cornell, Morrison taught English at Texas Southern University in Houston and then returned to Howard University to teach. Her students at Howard included Stokely Carmichael, later a leader in the Civil Rights movement, and Claude Brown, who asked her to read a draft of his novel *Manchild in the Promised Land* (1965), later published to wide acclaim.

While teaching at Howard, Morrison met and married Harold Morrison, a Jamaican-born architect. Their first son, Harold Ford, was born in 1962. During this time, Morrison also joined a writing group, in which the members exchanged and commented upon one another's work. For one of the meetings, she wrote a short story about an African American girl who wishes for blue eyes, a story she would later expand into her first novel, *The Bluest Eye* (1970).

In 1964, pregnant with her second son, Slade, Morrison separated from her husband, left her teaching job at Howard University, and returned to her hometown of Lorain, Ohio. The Morrisons later divorced.

HIGHLIGHTS IN MORRISON'S LIFE

1931 Toni Morrison is born Chloe Anthony Wofford on February 18 in Lorain, Ohio.

1953 Graduates from Howard University with a major in English.

1955 Earns master's degree from Cornell University; begins teaching English at Texas Southern University and later at Howard University.

1958 Marries Harold Morrison.

1962 First son, Harold, is born.

1964 Second son, Slade, is born; Morrison separates from husband.

1965 Morrison takes a job editing textbooks for a division of Random House in Syracuse, New York.

1967 Transfers to New York City to edit for trade division of Random House.

1970 Publishes first novel, *The Bluest Eye*.

1973 Publishes *Sula*, which is nominated for the National Book Award.

1977 Publishes *Song of Solomon*, which wins the National Book Critics Circle Award.

1981 Publishes *Tar Baby*; is pictured on cover of *Newsweek*.

1986 Her play, *Dreaming Emmett*, is performed in New York and wins the New York State Governor's Art Award.

1987 Morrison publishes *Beloved* to popular and critical acclaim.

1988 Wins Pulitzer Prize in fiction for *Beloved*; begins teaching at Princeton University.

1992 Publishes *Jazz*, a novel, and *Playing in the Dark: Whiteness and the Literary Imagination*, a work of literary criticism.

1993 Receives Nobel Prize in Literature.

1998 Film version of *Beloved*, directed by Jonathan Demme and starring Oprah Winfrey, is released.

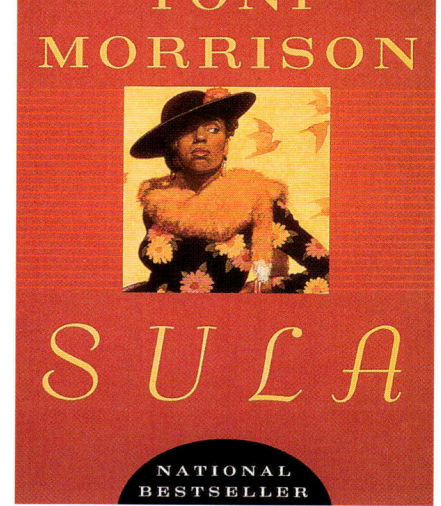

Morrison's eye is always trained on the collective African American past, on slavery and its long legacy. It is part of her story and the story of millions more. Artist and photographer Ben Shahn's 1935 photograph, entitled *Cotton Picking, Pulaski County, Arkansas*, captures the often harsh reality of the rural poor forced to labor in the Deep South.

Two New Careers. In the following year Morrison took a job as a textbook editor for a division of Random House in Syracuse, New York. There, she began writing at night after her children went to bed, expanding one of her short stories into the novel *The Bluest Eye*, which was finally published in 1970 after being rejected by several publishers.

Meanwhile, Morrison had been transferred from the textbook to the trade division of Random House, moving to New York City in 1967. There she edited the autobiography of boxer Muhammad Ali, *The Greatest: My Own Story* (1975), as well as *The Black Book: Three Hundred Years of African American Life* (1974), an anthology documenting the lives of African Americans in the United States. She also worked with African American writers Gayl Jones and Toni Cade Bambara. Even if she had never written her own novels, Toni Morrison's impact on African American literature would be significant.

Recognition as a Writer. As Morrison's success as an editor grew, so did her success as a writer. In 1973 her second novel, *Sula*, was released to highly positive reviews and a National Book Award nomination. *Song of Solomon* followed in 1977. It won the National Book Critics Circle Award in fiction and was chosen as a main selection of the Book-of-the-Month Club, the first book by an African American chosen for this honor since Richard Wright's *Native Son* in 1940. The publication of *Tar Baby* in 1981 won Morrison a place on the cover of *Newsweek*, making her only the second African American woman to appear there.

Seeing her face gracing the covers of magazines was nothing new to Morrison by the time her seventh novel, *Paradise*, was released in 1998.

in 1986 and won the New York State Governor's Art Award.

Morrison's Trilogy. At this time, Morrison began work on what she envisioned as a three-part novel, set in three different time periods. This project evolved into a trilogy, each book depicting a significant period of African American history. In the first novel, *Beloved*, Morrison deals with slavery.

A group of African American writers and scholars published a protest in *The New York Times Book Review* when *Beloved* won neither the National Book Award nor the National Book Critics Circle Award in 1988. However, the novel won the Pulitzer Prize for fiction a few months later. The 1998 film version of *Beloved*, directed by Jonathan Demme and starring Oprah Winfrey, drew new readers to Morrison's work.

The second novel of the trilogy, *Jazz*, appeared in 1992. It is set in Harlem during the 1920s, a vibrant and productive period in African American literature and arts known as the Harlem Renaissance. *Paradise*, the final installment, followed in 1998.

Morrison effectively juggled her editing job, teaching positions, novel writing, and raising two sons alone. She has said she was able to accomplish all this by having a limited social life. She wrote in the room where her sons played, because she found they interrupted her less often than if she wrote in a room alone. Morrison left editing in 1983 to devote more time to writing but continued teaching university writing courses. In 1984 she was named the Albert Schweitzer Professor of the Humanities at the State University of New York. Her unpublished play, *Dreaming Emmett*, was performed there This third novel in Morrison's trilogy depicts life in an all-black town in Oklahoma during the 1970s.

Nobel Prize and Beyond. In 1993 Morrison was awarded the Nobel Prize in Literature, the highest honor that can be bestowed upon a writer. Shortly afterward, a fire damaged her house on the Hudson River in New York, where she had done much of her work. In 1988 she began teaching at Princeton University, where she holds the Robert F. Goheen Professorship in the Humanities. She became the first African American woman to hold a named chair at an Ivy League university.

The Writer's Work

By 1998 Toni Morrison had written seven novels, a play, a volume of literary criticism, a children's book, book reviews, and commentaries. She is known, however, primarily for her novels, which depict the experiences of African Americans from slavery to the present. Her portrayals of women characters are particularly significant, as many of the most famous African American writers—Richard Wright, Ralph Ellison, and James Baldwin among them—have focused primarily on male characters.

Racial Issues. African Americans' dealings with racism and separation from mainstream white culture—from the era of slavery to the present day—are central issues in Morrison's novels. Morrison is a self-consciously black writer, making black characters central in all her fiction. Her language derives from African American culture. She includes black idioms and effectively renders dialogue. In addition, her writing employs the rhythms of oral storytelling, music, and the sermon—all important and well-developed forms in African American

On one hand, Morrison's word is an attempt to portray African American life and present it, uncensored, to an African American audience. Like the novelist, the painter Archibald Motley rendered people as active, vibrant individuals and not stereotypes, as in his 1935 painting *Saturday Night* (Howard University Gallery of Art, Washington, D.C.).

culture. Most important, Morrison envisions her audience as African American. Her specific focus allows her to treat her subject matter with exceptional depth.

In her novels, Morrison neither simplifies racial issues nor relies on stereotypes for character development. In her complex portrayals of characters, persons of any race may be heroic or cruel. For example, in *Beloved*, white characters make survival possible for escaped slaves. Amy, a young girl, helps to deliver the slave Sethe's baby, born during Sethe's flight to freedom. Amy finds Sethe a place to hide until she is strong enough to travel. In Cincinnati, whites help the escaped slaves find work and homes. Even among the slaveholders, there are differences in behavior. For example, Mr. Garner asks his slaves' opinions and allows Halle to work extra hours to buy his mother, Baby Suggs, out of slavery. On the other hand, Schoolteacher is deliberately cruel, testing the slaves' responses to ill treatment.

The African American characters also vary in virtue. Sethe's neighbors hold a grudge against Sethe and her family for years out of their jealousy over a party to which Sethe's family treated the neighborhood. However, these neighbors can also be helpful and kind, feeding people who need food and giving them a place to stay when they need one.

In *Playing in the Dark: Whiteness and the Literary Imagination* Morrison argues that race is a central theme in American literature, even when black characters do not appear in the works. She poses the questions of how racism affects white writers and how it shapes the dominant white culture. The issue of race is always present in Morrison's work, as her black characters work to navigate that culture.

Women's Issues. Morrison has criticized the women's movement for focusing mainly on white, middle-class women. Her books portray the difficulty of being female and African American and highlight the importance of friendships between women. She has argued that black women have always needed and helped one another. She has also stated that in her childhood family, tasks were not divided by gender roles. Instead, all family members did whatever needed to be done.

Race and gender are just two of the filters through which the voice of Morrison, seen here at home in 1992, travels.

SOME INSPIRATIONS BEHIND MORRISON'S WORK

Toni Morrison grew up in a family that stressed the importance of a good education and encouraged her to read at an early age. She was able to read before starting first grade and was an avid reader throughout her childhood. Her reading included many classic works of literature, including Gustave Flaubert's *Madame Bovary* (1857), the novels of Jane Austen, and works by twentieth-century American writers such as Ernest Hemingway and William Faulkner. As an undergraduate and graduate student studying English, Morrison continued to read extensively. Her master's thesis on suicide in the works of Faulkner and Virginia Woolf enabled her to study those authors in particular depth. Morrison's writing is frequently compared to Faulkner's in its richness of language and complexity of narrative.

Stories from African American folklore were popular in Morrison's childhood household. Morrison incorporates such tales in her fiction, and the supernatural elements such as the ghost in *Beloved*, the stories of people who can fly in *Song of Solomon*, and the Br'er Rabbit story that provides the title for *Tar Baby* come from this tradition.

Morrison became conscious of race issues early in life. Her father distrusted all whites and believed them incapable of overcoming racism. Because she lived in a mixed neighborhood and attended school with mostly white children, Morrison learned about race relations at first hand. For the most part, black and white members of her community got along; however, racism was prevalent. For example, blacks were not allowed on the public beach in Lorain, Ohio.

Morrison's native Ohio is the setting for several of her novels. *The Bluest Eye* takes place in Lorain, *Sula* in a fictional Ohio town, and *Beloved* in Cincinnati. Settings that are neither the Deep South nor the inner city enable Morrison to avoid some of the stereotypes associated with African Americans.

The stories told in the Morrison household planted a seed in the mind of the aspiring writer and suggested the power and legacy of creating tales of her own. In his 1970 work *Patchwork Quilt* (The Museum of Modern Art, New York), Romare Bearden alludes to the rich tradition of quilting. To some African American seamstresses, the bold shapes and intricate patterns of cloth created a form of storytelling as well.

Most of Morrison's novels have female protagonists. *The Bluest Eye* describes a young African American girl's struggle with the prevailing standard for beauty in American culture. Barraged by images such as pictures of Shirley Temple, Pecola Breedlove longs for the blue eyes which she believes will make her beautiful.

Sula portrays the friendship of two women, which is broken only when one has an affair with the other's husband. Even after this incident, Nel Wright never stops missing her friend, Sula Peace.

In *Beloved*, Sethe is willing to kill her children to keep them from being slaves. The strength of maternal love is a central theme in the novel; slavery's destruction of motherhood stands out as one of the institution's greatest tragedies. Sethe, her ghostly daughter, Beloved, and her living daughter, Denver, love and need one another. In one section of the novel the thoughts and conversations of all three appear in such a way that it is not always possible to tell who is speaking; the women are so interconnected that it does not matter.

Paradise portrays the healing and comfort possible in a community of women. A group of women invent new rituals for healing the pain of their difficult lives. The novel states that one of the women is white but never reveals which one. In this subtle manner, Morrison makes clear that certain problems faced by women are not limited to black women—that race does not always matter.

Literary Influences. Many elements in Morrison's work echo those of African American folklore. For example, many folk legends tell of slaves who can fly, and this motif appears in *Song of Solomon*. The title *Tar Baby* comes from a Br'er Rabbit story, the most commonly read version being the one recorded by Joel Chandler Harris, in his *Uncle Remus: His Songs and His Sayings* (1880). Ghosts are common in this folklore; the novel *Beloved* is named for a ghost, who is one of the central characters.

Morrison's work is often discussed in the context of Magical Realism as well. Magical Realism is the term used to describe the inclusion of supernatural elements in the works of Latin American writers, particularly Gabriel García Márquez and Isabel Allende. In their works, ghosts and other phenomena serve as plot elements but also function metaphorically to illuminate the themes and realistic occurrences in the works. For example, the ghost in *Beloved* is an actual ghost seen by many characters in the novel. At the same time, it represents the haunting presence of slavery remaining in the lives of ex-slaves.

Morrison's rich language, complex sentence structure, and masterful interweaving of voices and time frames evoke the work of William Faulkner and Virginia Woolf, whom she studied in depth in graduate school. As Morrison's career progressed, her language became increasingly descriptive, metaphorical, and musical.

BIBLIOGRAPHY

Bloom, Harold, ed. *Toni Morrison*. New York: Chelsea House, 1990.

Century, Douglas. *Toni Morrison*. New York: Chelsea House, 1994.

Denard, Carolyn C. "Toni Morrison." In *Modern American Women Writers*, edited by Elaine Showalter. New York: Charles Scribner's Sons, 1991.

Gates, Henry Louis, Jr., and K. A. Appiah. *Toni Morrison: Critical Perspectives Past and Present*. New York: Amistad, 1993.

Kramer, Barbara. *Toni Morrison: Nobel Prize-Winning Author*. Springfield: N.J.: Enslow, 1996.

Kubitschek, Missy Dehn. *Toni Morrison: A Critical Companion*. Westport, Conn.: Greenwood Press, 1998.

Patrick-Wexler, Diane. *Toni Morrison*. Austin: Raintree Steck-Vaughn, 1997.

Peach, Linden. *Toni Morrison*. New York: St. Martin's Press, 1995.

Rigney, Barbara Hill. *The Voices of Toni Morrison*. Columbus: Ohio State University Press, 1991.

Taylor-Guthrie, Danille, ed. *Conversations with Toni Morrison*. Jackson: University of Mississippi Press, 1994.

Slavery in Beloved—The Facts Behind the Fiction

Although the main plot of *Beloved* (1987) takes place after African Americans were freed from slavery by the Emancipation Proclamation in 1863, the novel contains perhaps the most harrowing depiction of slave life in American literature. As the characters remember their lives and tell their stories, the book reveals the horror of slavery through vivid details. Toni Morrison demonstrates her ability to create a great story through her skill with language and

Margaret Garner, in this wood engraving made from a Thomas Nobel painting and first appearing in the May 18, 1867, edition of *Harper's Magazine*, stands over two of her children lying dead on the floor, killed by her own hand so that they would not have to live their lives as slaves. Her other two children cling to her skirt as she faces the slave catchers sent to retrieve her. Garner's remaining children were taken from her, and she would eventually commit suicide.

her careful research. The factual information provides a framework for the fiction; at the same time, the fictional narrative allows the reader to experience the painful reality of the historical truths.

The Margaret Garner Story. Morrison's inspiration for *Beloved* came from a newspaper story in an 1856 edition of *The American Baptist*. Like Sethe, the novel's protagonist, the historical Margaret Garner was an escaped slave living near Cincinnati, Ohio, with her four children. According to the federal Fugitive Slave Law of 1850, slaveholders could capture runaway slaves even in free states. When slave hunters found Garner, she tried to kill her children, believing that death was better than life in slavery. She killed one and wounded the others. Abolitionists took up Garner's cause, publicizing her story as evidence that if a mother would go to such extreme lengths to protect her children from slavery, the institution must be abolished.

Morrison encountered this newspaper article while editing *The Black Book: Three Hundred Years of African American Life* (1974), a history of African American experience in America. The story for *Beloved* began with this true account; Morrison even used Garner's last name as the name for the slave owners at the Sweet Home plantation in *Beloved*. However, Morrison did not attempt extensive research on Margaret Garner. Instead, she wanted to imagine on her own the details that would bring the story to life.

III Treatment of Slaves.

The pre–Civil War laws of the slave-holding states defined slaves both as property and as persons. The laws varied over time and among states, but, in practice, they protected the property rights of the slave owners above the personal rights of the slaves. All slave codes ensured the rights of slaveholders to discipline their property. Slaves were beaten, chained, shackled, branded, and maimed at the will of their owners.

In *Beloved*, the slave owners beat, rape, and even kill their slaves. Scars in the shape of a tree cover Sethe's back, the result of a beating she received. Her most horrifying memory of her slave days is of two teenage boys sucking the milk from her breasts, a torture supervised by the plantation foreman.

Beyond physical pain, slavery imposed great psychological harm on the slaves. One of the worst effects of slavery was the destruction of family life among slaves. Because slaves could be sold at any time, any family bonds among them were temporary. Some slaveholders allowed their slaves to marry, while others did not; even the marriages that were permitted could be dissolved if the owner decided to sell one or more spouse.

Slaves reproduced for the slaveholders' profit rather than to create families. Children could be sold or taken from their mothers. In the novel, Sethe sees

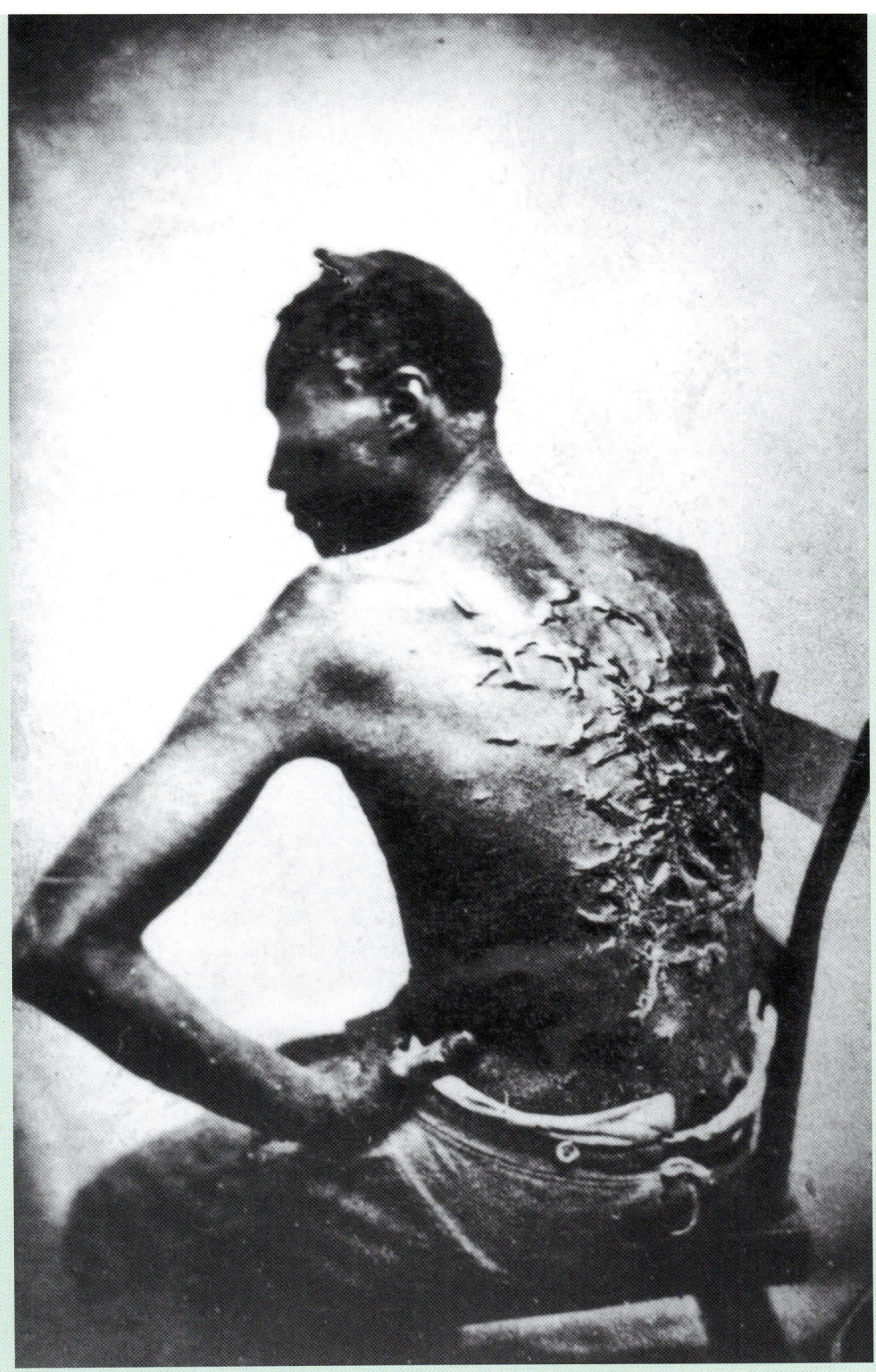
This 1870s photograph reveals a slave's back laced with scars, a testament to a history of unthinkable abuse.

her mother only a few times even though they live at the same plantation. Her mother works all day in the fields, and one slave is assigned care of the slave children. Baby Suggs, Sethe's mother-in-law, sees only one of her eight children to adulthood.

Instruments of Torture. Some of the most shocking scenes in *Beloved* describe tortures performed on the slaves. Morrison traveled as far as Brazil to see punishment devices used on slaves that she had not seen in museums in the United States. For example, she had read in slaveholders' diaries about using something called "the bit" on slaves. She learned that the bit had a metal plate that covered the tongue, and pieces that wrapped around the head could be tightened. Slaves were unable to speak when wearing it. The bit was very painful not only when it was being worn but also for days afterward. In *Beloved*, the plantation foreman at Sweet Home uses this device on the slaves.

The foreman also puts a three-spoke collar on one of the slaves. With the long metal spokes protruding from such a collar, one could neither lie down nor lean against a wall nor even shake one's head while wearing it. The device made comfort or sleep impossible.

Monument to the Slaves. Morrison dedicated *Beloved* to "Sixty Million and more"—an allusion to the sixty million Africans she believes were taken from Africa by the Atlantic slave trade. Slave traders packed into their ships as many as twice the number of slaves they promised to deliver. Many slaves perished during trip across the ocean as a result of starvation and disease spread by unsanitary conditions. Beatings and rape were common on the slave-trading vessels. Morrison's *Beloved* is a powerful monument both to those who died under slavery and to those who lived to tell their stories.

SOURCES FOR FURTHER STUDY

Berlin, Ira, Marc Favreau, and Steven F. Miller, eds. *Remembering Slavery: African Americans Talk About Their Personal Experiences of Slavery*. New York: The New Press, 1998.

Harris, Trudier. "Escaping Slavery but Not Its Images." In *Toni Morrison: Critical Perspectives Past and Present*, edited by Henry Louis Gates, Jr., and K. A. Appiah. New York: Amistad, 1993.

Stampp, Kenneth M. *The Peculiar Institution: Slavery in the Ante-Bellum South*. New York: Vintage, 1956.

Reader's Guide to Major Works

BELOVED

Genre: Novel
Subgenre: Historical drama and supernatural thriller
Published: New York, 1987
Time period: Reconstruction era, with flashbacks to pre–Civil War slave times
Setting: Cincinnati, Ohio; Sweet Home plantation in Kentucky

Themes and Issues. *Beloved* is at once both an enthralling ghost story and a painfully realistic account of slavery and its effects. In order to maintain the myths that make slavery possible, the owners treat their slaves like animals. Slaves are considered property to be bred and sold. As Toni Morrison noted, slavery depended upon the absence of families. Further, the slave owners could use or harm slaves as they saw fit: They could breed them for future profit or abuse them severely. One form of abuse was "the bit," a torture device placed in slaves' mouths so that they could not talk. The device was painful, even deadly, both while it was being worn and afterward.

The Plot. Sethe and her daughter Denver live in a house haunted by the ghost of Sethe's baby daughter, whose tombstone is engraved with the word "Beloved." The neighbors shun the two because of the ghost and because of their family history. Paul D, an old friend from the same plantation as Sethe, arrives one day and stays. One day, a young woman appears at the

Actresses Thandie Newton, Oprah Winfrey, and Kimberly Elise starred in the 1998 film adaptation of *Beloved*, in which the horrors of slavery and the mistakes of the past threaten the healing of a broken family.

house, calling herself "Beloved." She is the age that Sethe's dead daughter would be, had she lived, and she has a scar on her neck.

Beloved demands as much of Sethe's time as she can get, and Sethe gradually believes she is her dead daughter in human form. Paul D leaves the women when he learns that Sethe killed her daughter.

Years before, slave hunters found Sethe and her four children after their escape from slavery. Rather than returning to life as a slave and subjecting her children to the same existence, Sethe tried to kill the children before the slave hunters could catch them. She succeeded in slitting one daughter's throat before a friend stopped her from killing Denver, her newborn daughter, and two sons.

After Paul D's departure, Sethe and Beloved become interested only in one another, to the point that Sethe stops going to work on time and gets fired. With no food in the house, Denver ventures out and asks neighbors for work and help. The neighbors bring food to the women, and Denver finds a job caring for an elderly couple at night. The women of the community decide to run the ghost out and meet outside the house to pray. With Beloved gone, Paul D returns to Sethe.

Analysis. *Beloved* poignantly depicts the devastation caused by slavery. By focusing on the experiences of one ex-slave, Morrison treats her subject matter with great depth. The novel contrasts the view of the slave owners toward Sethe with the reality of her humanity. The slave owners see Sethe as a piece of property useful for performing household tasks and for breeding new property, in her babies, who can then be sold.

In fact, Sethe loves her children as much as any mother can love. She would rather kill her children than let them live as slaves. She remembers little of her own mother, who worked all day in the fields until she was hanged with a group of other slaves. Sethe never learned why her mother was killed and does not want her children to be taken from her as her mother was. Her most devastating experience as a slave was Schoolteacher's nephews taking the milk from her breasts—milk meant for her child. Morrison was inspired to write *Beloved* by reading about Margaret Garner, an escaped slave who tried to kill her children rather than see them returned to slavery.

The events in the novel do not occur in chronological order but instead are revealed as various characters remember them. This method

LONG FICTION

- 1970 The Bluest Eye
- 1973 Sula
- 1977 Song of Solomon
- 1981 Tar Baby
- 1987 Beloved
- 1992 Jazz
- 1998 Paradise

CHILDREN'S LITERATURE

- 1999 The Big Box (with Slade Morrison and Giselle Potter)

NONFICTION

- 1992 Playing in the Dark: Whiteness and the Literary Imagination
- 1997 Birth of a Nation'hood: Gaze, Script, and Spectacle in the O. J. Simpson Case

EDITED TEXTS

- 1992 Race-ing Justice, En-gendering Power: Essays on Anita Hill, Clarence Thomas, and the Construction of Social Reality

PLAYS

- 1986 Dreaming Emmett

of storytelling adds to the novel's emotional impact; the reader learns not only what happens but also what the characters think and feel about present and past events.

SOURCES FOR FURTHER STUDY

Atwood, Margaret. "Haunted by Their Nightmares." In *Toni Morrison*, edited by Harold Bloom. New York: Chelsea House, 1990.

Harris, Trudier. "Escaping Slavery but Not Its Images." In *Toni Morrison: Critical Perspectives Past and Present*, edited by Henry Louis Gates, Jr., and K. A. Appiah. New York: Amistad, 1993.

Mobley, Marilyn Sanders. "A Different Remembering: Memory, History, and Meaning in Toni Morrison's *Beloved*." In *Toni Morrison*, edited by Harold Bloom. New York, Chelsea House, 1990.

THE BLUEST EYE

Genre: Novel
Subgenre: Social criticism
Published: New York, 1970
Time period: 1940–1941
Setting: Lorain, Ohio

Themes and Issues. The young African American girls in *The Bluest Eye* struggle against a culture that defines them as unattractive or invisible, in contrast with the white film star Shirley Temple and the white baby dolls they are given as gifts and expected to love. Claudia MacTeer dismembers her dolls, trying to find out what inside them makes them so beautiful to the adults who give them to her. Pecola Breedlove prays for blue eyes, which she believes will make her beautiful.

The Plot. Eleven-year-old Pecola Breedlove stays with the MacTeer family after her father, Cholly, sets fire to the Breedlove's apartment. Her friends Claudia and Frieda try to make her feel at home there. Pecola loves to drink from their Shirley Temple cup, because she loves the picture of the starlet on the side of it. Claudia, the narrator of this part of the novel, hates Shirley Temple and also hates the white baby dolls she is given for Christmas and expected to love.

After Pecola goes back to live with her family, her father rapes her. She becomes pregnant. In her misery, all she can think about is how much she wants blue eyes so that she will be beautiful; she believes her problems will disappear if her eyes turn blue. She visits Soaphead Church, a spiritualist, to ask for blue eyes. He gives her a piece of poisoned meat to give to his landlady's dog and tells her that if the dog acts strangely after eating it, Pecola will get her wish. Pecola watches the dog die. She goes insane, convinced that her

The Bluest Eye presents a world seen partially through the sad eyes of a little girl whose turbid environment makes her old beyond her years. William H. Johnson's 1944 oil painting *Li'l Sis* (Smithsonian American Art Museum, Washington, D.C) presents a similar figure unable to fully inhabit the frivolity of childhood.

eyes have turned blue. Her baby is born prematurely and dies.

Claudia and Frieda feel sorry for Pecola and try to help her by burying money they have earned to buy a bicycle. However, even Claudia eventually learns to love Shirley Temple; her resistance to white ideals of beauty breaks down.

Analysis. The novel begins with a passage from an elementary school reading primer about the characters Dick and Jane. The passage is repeated without punctuation and capitalization and then again with the words run together. The chapters begin with short sections of this passage, again with the words run together, and sometimes ending in the middle of a word. The passages from the reader describe a white family with a pretty house, a smiling father, a laughing mother, and a daughter who sees a friend who will play with her. The family of this passage contrasts with the Breedlove family, who live in an ugly apartment above a furniture store, are very unhappy, and do not know how to improve their lives.

Morrison's inclusion of the passage from the reader introduces the theme of ideals from popular culture that do not match the reality of the black characters' lives. The black women give their daughters white baby dolls and Shirley Temple tea sets. They admire white girls they see instead of finding beauty in their own children. Before her children were born, Mrs. Breedlove went to the movies frequently, yearning for the kind of life and beauty she saw on the screen. Pecola, ignored and mistreated by everyone except the MacTeer girls who befriend her, believes that if she were more beautiful, the problems of her life would disappear; her idea of beauty is having blue eyes.

SOURCES FOR FURTHER STUDY

Gibson, Donald B. "Text and Countertext in *The Bluest Eye*." In *Toni Morrison: Critical Perspectives Past and Present*, edited by Henry Louis Gates, Jr., and K. A. Appiah. New York: Amistad, 1993.

Harris, Trudier. "Reconnecting Fragments: Afro-American Folk Tradition in *The Bluest Eye*." In *Critical Essays on Toni Morrison*, edited by Nellie Y. McKay. Boston: G. K. Hall, 1988.

Miner, Madonne M. "Lady No Longer Sings the Blues: Rape, Madness, and Silence in *The Bluest Eye*." In *Toni Morrison*, edited by Harold Bloom. New York: Chelsea House, 1990.

SONG OF SOLOMON
Genre: Novel
Subgenre: *Bildungsroman*
Published: New York, 1977
Time period: 1930s to 1960s
Setting: Detroit, Michigan; Shalimar, Virginia

Themes and Issues. The title *Song of Solomon* refers to a circle-game song that children sing in the book. Although Milkman does not understand the song when he first hears it, it tells the story of his ancestors. According to local legend, his great-grandfather could fly, and one day he flew away, leaving his wife and twenty-one children behind. The flying motif is common in African American folklore; slaves were believed to have flown back to Africa. Milkman has had a lifelong interest in flying; by the end of the novel he learns that there are ways to fly without ever leaving the ground.

The Plot. Milkman Dead's mother, Ruth, is the daughter of a well-respected doctor, and his father, Macon, owns rental properties. Macon Dead is an extremely greedy man who dislikes his wife. Ruth, in her loneliness, breast-feeds her son until he is quite old. The neighborhood gossip sees this and gives the boy the nickname "Milkman."

Milkman is a lonely boy until he befriends an older boy named Guitar. Together, the two boys go the home of Milkman's aunt, Pilate. She lives with her daughter and granddaughter, with whom she makes and sells wine. Milkman's father has forbidden him to have any contact with Pilate. However, Milkman is intrigued by her and falls in love with her granddaughter, his cousin Hagar.

Milkman grows up and helps his father in his business. He continues his relationship with Hagar and has other girlfriends as well. After many years, he decides that he is bored with Hagar and writes her a note telling her he does not want to see her again. Hagar is heartbroken, and once a month she tries to kill Milkman.

Meanwhile, Milkman learns that Guitar has joined a group of seven men called the Days. Every time a black person is killed by a white person who is not brought to justice, the Days execute a white person in a manner similar to that in which the black person was murdered.

Milkman's father, Macon, believes that his sister Pilate has a sack of gold in her house and wants Milkman to steal it. Milkman invites Guitar to help and to share the money. Guitar needs money for the Days' activities and agrees. The two young men steal the bag, which they think contains gold. They are stopped by police, who search their car and discover that the bag is full of human bones. Pilate rescues Milkman and Guitar from jail with a story that the bones are her husband's bones, which she could not afford to bury.

Years before, Pilate and Macon had killed a man in a cave full of gold. The ghost of Pilate's father told her to collect the bones and take them away, so she went back for them a few years later. Milkman goes to Danville, Pennsylvania, to search for the cave to see if the gold is still there. He finds the cave but not the gold.

Milkman then heads for Virginia, thinking Pilate might have taken the gold there. Instead, he finds the place where his ancestors lived and learns the local legend that his great-grandfather could fly. He also learns that, after his father had buried his grandfather, the bones had washed up and were placed in the cave where the gold had been. Milkman realizes that someone else had been to the cave before Pilate returned to it and taken the gold as well as the body of the man Macon had killed. The bones that Pilate kept in the bag were those of her father. While Milkman is in Virginia, Guitar tracks him down and tries to kill him, thinking he has the gold.

While Milkman is traveling, Hagar, still distraught over Milkman's loss of interest in her,

Like Morrison's *Song of Solomon*, Charles White's 1971 work *Wanted, Poster Series # 17* (Flint Institute of Arts, Flint, Michigan) explores issues of guilt, criminality, and who should bear the responsibility for grievous deeds committed in the past. White used old wanted posters seeking runaway slaves as the backdrop for his scene of a slave mother about to be sold and separated from her child. Although Morrison's vigilantes are never given her full endorsement in the novel, they allow her to examine the issue of culpability in instances of racism and racial violence.

becomes ill and dies. Milkman, much wiser, realizes that he is responsible. He takes Pilate to Virginia to bury her father's bones. During the burial, Guitar shoots and kills Pilate. Milkman dares Guitar to kill him, and then jumps from a cliff, flying at last. The ending leaves readers uncertain whether Milkman lives or dies.

Analysis. Milkman's journey south teaches him values that counter his father's love of money and Guitar's belief in the righteousness of random violence. He learns to appreciate his family's history and even comes to think more positively about his father, after talking to people who knew him as a boy.

Milkman's knowledge brings a newfound respect for names. His grandfather had been renamed "Macon Dead" by a drunk bureaucrat who wrote responses in the wrong boxes on a form—the grandfather had been born in Macon and his father was dead. Except for the firstborn sons, all of whom are named Macon, members of the Dead family are named by choosing names from the Bible at random. Thus, Milkman's aunt is named Pilate and his sisters are named Magdalena and First Corinthians. Like Pilate, who carries a scrap of paper with her name on it in a box hanging from her ear, Milkman learns that names matter. The official names for people and places and the new names given because of events or even mistakes all tell stories and add layers of meaning.

Song of Solomon raises the issue of effective ways to deal with racism. Guitar's group, the Days, fights violence with equivalent violence. Milkman believes that Guitar's violence is unfair and will solve nothing. In fact, Guitar becomes so caught up in violence that he needlessly kills Pilate.

SOURCES FOR FURTHER STUDY

Mason, Theodore O., Jr. "The Novelist as Conservator: Stories and Comprehension in Toni Morrison's *Song of Solomon*." In *Toni Morrison*, edited by Harold Bloom. New York: Chelsea House, 1990.

Mobley, Marilyn Sanders. *Folk Roots and Mythic Wings in Sarah Orne Jewett and Toni Morrison: The Cultural Function of Narrative*. Baton Rouge: Louisiana State University Press, 1991.

O'Shaughnessy, Kathleen. "'Life Life Life Life': The Community as Chorus in *Song of Solomon*." In *Critical Essays on Toni Morrison*, edited by Nellie Y. McKay. Boston: G. K. Hall, 1988.

Other Works

JAZZ (1992). The second novel in the trilogy begun by *Beloved* and ended by *Paradise*, *Jazz* takes its inspiration from historical events surrounding a young woman's murder during the Harlem Renaissance of the 1920s, a period of great artistic and literary achievement that centered on African Americans living in the Harlem area of New York City. Morrison based her story on that of a young woman whose photograph appears in the photographer James Van Der Zee's *The Harlem Book of the Dead* (1978), a collection of funeral photographs documenting life in Harlem during the 1920s.

In the novel, Joe Trace has an affair with a young woman named Dorcas. When she leaves him for a younger man, he kills her. Joe's wife, Violet, tries to stab Dorcas's corpse at the funeral. Her later attempts at revenge include having an affair of her own and finding out all she can about Dorcas by befriending the dead woman's friends, among other things.

The novel has an unusual first-person narrator whose identity is never revealed. The narrator speaks as an observer rather than a participant in the action but reveals enough personal information to suggest that he or she may be unreliable.

Jazz, the musical form from which the novel takes its title, became popular during the 1920s. Morrison's writing style has frequently been described as musical. In this novel, her language and sentence structure are more elaborate than ever, perhaps approximating the complexity of jazz music.

PARADISE (1998). The third novel in the trilogy that includes *Beloved* and *Jazz*, *Paradise* is set in the 1970s and juxtaposes two communi-

portrayed—blacks and women. The massacre at the Convent divides the town: Many of the town's women are sympathetic with the women of the Convent, while some of the men remain concerned about keeping control and wish to eliminate anything that might threaten them.

The novel begins, "They shoot the white girl first," yet the reader never learns which of the women staying at the Convent is white. Morrison has noted that she meant to leave this point ambiguous: It does not matter whether the women are black or white.

SULA (1973). *Sula* tells the stories of two women friends, Nel Wright and Sula Peace, from their childhoods onward. The novel spans a period from 1919 to 1965 and depicts these very different women as they grow to adulthood. Nel marries, has children, and lives a conventional life. Sula, on the other hand, leaves the neighborhood for a number of years. When she comes back, she lives as she pleases: She has no interest in marriage, puts her mother in a nursing home, and has an affair with Nel's husband. This affair ends the women's friendship. Years after Sula's death, Nel realizes how badly she has missed her girlhood friend, when she believed she was missing her husband.

This novel is significant in its central focus on the friendship of two African American women. That friendship is a lasting and crucial part of both women's lives. Morrison does not judge the two women or the choices they make. Both Nel's narrow conventionality and Sula's disregard for standards of behavior have limitations. At the end of the novel, Sula's grandmother, Eva, confuses Nel for Sula, and says there was never any difference between the two women. Nel realizes the truth of this statement. When they were children, Sula accidently threw a boy in the river. While he drowned, Nel watched calmly. Remembering that incident, Nel realizes that she had enjoyed the excitement, whereas Sula was deeply upset; clearly Nel was no better than her friend.

The novel begins with a discussion of the Bottom, the black neighborhood in Medallion,

In *Paradise* Morrison plays with various notions of sisterhood, between African American and white women and between nuns and the female residents of the town of Ruby. In this 1931 Doris Ulmann photograph, *Nun with Girl, New Orleans*, a woman devotes herself to the care of orphans.

ties that are refuges of sorts. Ruby, Oklahoma, is an all-black town in which the founders are protective of their isolation, racial purity, and traditional politics. The town's neighbors at the Convent, formerly a school run by nuns, are women who have drifted there escaping difficult pasts and abusive treatment by men. A group of men looking for someone to blame for the town's political tensions and perceived moral decline attack the Convent, killing the women. The bodies disappear, however, and four of the women later appear to family members of the townspeople.

In setting up a conflict between residents of an all-black town and a community of women, Morrison pits against one another members of two groups her novels have sympathetically

Ohio, that was actually a rocky hillside overlooking the fertile valley where the whites lived—the "bottom of Heaven" was the joke that gave the neighborhood its name. Morrison depicts the Bottom as a lively and beautiful community. Although the blacks live on the land the whites did not want, their neighborhood is eventually taken from them so the city can build a golf course. The community is literally destroyed for the pleasure of the white people of Medallion.

TAR BABY (1981). *Tar Baby*'s title comes from an African American folktale in which a farmer sets out a baby made of tar to trap Br'er Rabbit. Br'er Rabbit, the clever trickster, gets away from the tar baby. On the most simple level, Jadine—the African American niece of the servants Sydney and Ondine—is the tar baby, a creation of the white employer, Valerian Street, who paid for her education. Son, a politically charged but less-educated man who becomes romantically involved with Jadine, represents Br'er Rabbit and in fact ends the novel running away "lickety-split," just as Br'er Rabbit does.

Set mainly on the imaginary Caribbean island Isle des Chevaliers, *Tar Baby* is Morrison's only novel with significant white characters. The setting allows blacks and whites to argue their racial differences isolated from American culture. At the beginning of the novel, the social divisions between the Streets and their servants are clear. Son, who appears from nowhere, forces discussion of race.

Resources

No major archive of Toni Morrison's manuscripts and papers yet exists. Some sources of interest to students of Morrison include the following:

Toni Morrison Society. Based at Georgia State University in Atlanta, this organization is dedicated to the study of Morrison's work. The society holds a conference every other year to present new scholarships. (http://www.gsu.edu/~wwwtms/)

Toni Morrison Reading Room at the Lorain Public Library. The public library in Morrison's hometown of Lorain, Ohio, houses a comprehensive collection of materials by and about Morrison. Besides scholarly materials, the collection includes autographed first editions and foreign-language editions of Morrison's novels. Artworks depicting Morrison are displayed, as are magazine and newspaper articles about Morrison and her family. (http://www.lorain.lib.oh.us/localauthors/morrison.html)

Anniina's Toni Morrison Page. This Web site provides links to many of the most useful Morrison Web sites, categorized by biography, interpretation of individual novels, bibliography, and so forth. (http://www.luminarium.org/contemporary/tonimorrison/toni:htm)

Nobel Prize Internet Archive. Part of a Web site with information on Nobel Prize winners, this page contains links provided by the creators as well as those added by Archive visitors. Although some of the links are out of date or no longer accessible, most contain valuable information for the study of Morrison and her works. (http://www.stockton.edu/~stk10886/1993a.html)

Toni Morrison. In this documentary film, produced and directed by Alan Benson in 1987 and available on videotape, Morrison discusses *Beloved*, including the factual background to the novel and the issues it raises. In addition, Morrison and two professional actors read passages from the novel, providing an excellent opportunity to hear the richness of its prose.

JOAN HOPE

Alice Munro

BORN: July 10, 1931, Wingham, Ontario, Canada
IDENTIFICATION: Late-twentieth-century Canadian author known for her remarkable mastery of the short story.

With the publication of her first book, *Dance of the Happy Shades* (1968), Alice Munro established a distinctive Canadian voice firmly rooted in the Lake Huron country of southwestern Ontario. Her early work explores the intimate experience of girls and women, eloquently addressing the ways in which their society seeks to control them and the price they pay if they fail to conform. Her later collections present a compelling argument in favor of the short story as the literary equal of the novel. Munro's stories are widely anthologized, and her books have earned numerous honors in Canada, the United States, the United Kingdom, and Australia. Her fiction has been translated into fourteen languages.

The Writer's Life

Alice Munro was born Alice Ann Laidlaw on July 10, 1931, in Wingham, Ontario, not far from the shores of Lake Huron. Her father, Robert Eric Laidlaw, raised silver foxes on his small farm. Her mother, Anne Chamney Laidlaw, a native of the Ottawa Valley, had taught elementary school before her marriage.

Childhood. Munro's family, which also included a younger sister and brother, struggled unsuccessfully with poverty during the Great Depression of the 1930s. Munro attended a shabby two-room primary school much like the one described in her novel *Who Do You Think You Are?* (1978, published in the United States as *The Beggar Maid: Stories of Flo and Rose*, 1979). During World War II, her mother developed a serious illness that was eventually diagnosed as Parkinson's disease. When the fox farm eventually failed in 1948, Munro's father was forced to seek odd jobs, including that of night watchman in a local foundry. He

Precocious and hungry for knowledge, Munro, much like the girl in Jean Puy's 1934 painting *Study or The Schoolgirl* (Musée d'Art Moderne de la Ville de Paris), diligently applied herself to her studies, rising above the limited educational opportunities offered her in her hometown.

later resumed farming by raising and selling turkeys.

References to the family's financial difficulties and her mother's declining health appear frequently in Munro's early fiction, which draws largely on her own experience. After her mother's death in 1959, Munro wrote one of her most powerful and personal stories, "The Peace of Utrecht," in which she attempted to come to terms with the painful and ambivalent mother-daughter relationship. The narrator of "The Ottawa Valley," in a similar situation, confesses, "The problem, the only problem, is my mother . . . she looms too close, just as she always did."

Writing Apprenticeship. Munro loved to read and dreamed of being a writer from the age of eleven. She has said that her early desire to imitate others marked her as a potential artist, as it does Rose, who eventually becomes an actress in *Who Do You Think You Are?* At fourteen, Munro began to write a gothic novel in the manner of Emily Brontë's *Wuthering Heights* (1847), but she set it in her hometown of Wingham. Later, in *Lives of Girls and Women* (1971), the young Del Jordan begins a similar story.

In the fall of 1949, assisted by a two-year scholarship, Munro enrolled in the University of Western Ontario at London, Ontario. Originally she had planned to major in journalism, but she quickly switched to English. She published three stories in *Folio*, the campus literary magazine. Yet even with a part-time library job, she did not have enough money to continue her education after the scholarship expired.

At the age of twenty, Munro married a fellow student, James Munro, the son of a prominent Toronto family. The gap between his upper-middle-class experience and her limited rural background is suggested by the ill-matched

The late 1970s saw the establishment of Munro's growing international reputation. Munro's 1994 collection of short stories, *Open Secrets*, further cemented the high regard in which she is held. Photographer Marion Ettlinger took this publicity photograph around the time *Open Secrets* was published.

young couples who appear in *Who Do You Think You Are?* and several early stories.

Complications. In her own life Munro was struggling to balance the roles of artist and of wife and mother. Her conflict is reflected in the struggles of many of her women characters. In 1953, the year in which she sold her first short story to *Mayfair* magazine, she gave birth to her first daughter, Sheila. Her second daughter, Jenny, was born four years later. During this time, Munro continued to publish stories in Canadian magazines. Some were later adapted for radio or television by the Canadian Broadcasting Corporation.

Writing Success. In 1968 Munro published her initial collection, *Dance of the Happy Shades*, which earned Canada's most prestigious literary honor, the Governor-General's Literary Award for fiction. Three years later, her only novel, *Lives of Girls and Women*, firmly established her reputation as an outstanding young author. Although she dedicated this book to her husband, its publication marked the end of their marriage.

A Time of Transition. In 1972 Munro and her two younger daughters returned to Ontario, where she briefly taught fiction at York University in Toronto. She left that job for the University of Western Ontario, where she served as writer-in-residence for a term and published a second collection of stories, *Something I've Been Meaning to Tell You: Thirteen Stories* (1974).

In 1976 Munro divorced her first husband and married Gerald Fremlin, a geographer and federal cartographer whom she had known in her university student days. In this same year her father died following heart surgery, an event that triggered her story "The Moons of Jupiter." Its acceptance by The *New Yorker* initiated a long-standing relationship with that publication, in which many of her following stories would be published. She was also awarded an honorary doctorate of letters from the University of Western Ontario.

Mature Life. Throughout the 1980s and 1990s Munro's reputation continued to flourish. She published her work in magazines and anthologies, releasing a new collection of stories every few years. *Who Do You Think You Are?* and *The Progress of Love* (1986) both received the Governor-General's Literary Award. Munro was selected for the first Marian Engel Award, given to a woman writer for a distinguished body of work. In addition, her brooding collection *Open Secrets: Stories* (1994) earned the W. H. Smith Award for the best book published in the United Kingdom in 1995.

Although Munro has preferred to avoid public appearances and book tours, she has ap-

Like many of the female writers of her generation, Munro struggled to rectify her varying roles as artist, mother, and wife. At times they enriched and balanced each other, while at others, they clashed and diverged. Here she is seen with her husband, Gerald Fremlin, in 1999.

After the Munros moved to Vancouver, British Columbia, in 1963, she continued to write and to work at the public library, while James became a department store executive. In Vancouver, Munro rented an office in order to write free of distraction, but her landlord began to harass her. The resulting story, "The Office," calls attention to the very real problems of women writers who are not taken seriously. She likewise felt stifled by the traditional culture she encountered in Vancouver and was much happier when she and her husband established a bookstore in nearby Victoria, British Columbia. Their third daughter, Andrea, was born in 1966.

HIGHLIGHTS IN MUNRO'S LIFE

1931 Alice Munro is born Alice Ann Laidlaw on July 10 in Wingham, Ontario.

1948 Father's fox farm fails.

1949 Munro enrolls at the University of Western Ontario; publishes stories in campus literary magazine.

1951 Marries James Munro.

1953 First daughter, Sheila, is born; Munro sells first story.

1957 Second daughter, Jenny, is born.

1959 Mother dies of Parkinson's disease; Munro writes "The Peace of Utrecht."

1966 Third daughter, Andrea, is born.

1968 Munro publishes first short story collection, *Dance of the Happy Shades*, which receives Governor-General's Literary Award.

1971 Publishes novel *Lives of Girls and Women*, which firmly establishes her reputation.

1972 Munro leaves disintegrating marriage; returns to Ontario.

1976 Divorces James Munro; marries Gerald Fremlin; father dies.

1978 Munro publishes *Who Do You Think You Are?* (published in United States as *The Beggar Maid: Stories of Flo and Rose*, 1979), which receives Governor-General's Literary Award.

1979 Begins extensive travel through Australia, China, and Scandinavia.

1980 Writer-in-residence at the University of British Columbia, Vancouver, and the University of Queensland in Brisbane, Australia.

1986 Publishes *The Progress of Love*; receives Governor-General's Award and Marian Engel Award.

1997 Receives the PEN/Malamud Award for excellence in short fiction.

1998 *The Love of a Good Woman: Stories* receives Giller Prize for best work of fiction published in Canada, the only short-story collection to be considered.

1999 Munro receives National Book Critics Circle Award in fiction for *The Love of a Good Woman*.

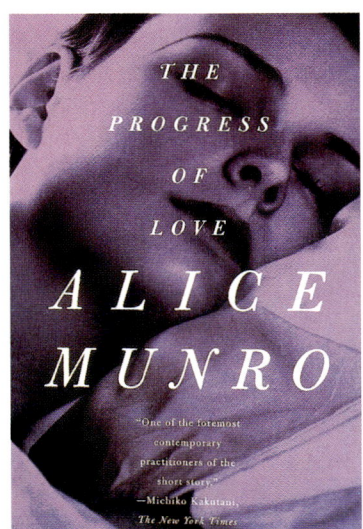

peared as an amateur actress in fundraisers for a local theater near Clinton, Ontario, where she settled with Fremlin in the house where he was born. The couple have also maintained a winter home in Comax on Vancouver Island in British Columbia.

The Writer's Work

Alice Munro's books consist of largely unrelated stories, although certain themes and character types reappear throughout her fiction. Even the interrelated chapters of *Lives of Girls and Women* have been published as separate stories. She indicated that she wanted her stories to give the reader "intense, but not connected, moments of experience" because that is how she saw life, as fragments rather than as a continuum.

Issues in Munro's Fiction. Munro's work is characterized by an unflinching examination of all aspects of female experience in modern life. At the same time, Munro explores the manner in which a rigid society can damage its members by restricting them to arbitrary gender or economic roles. She is not so much a reformer or even a social commentator as she is an observer, and what she observes so closely is the unchallenged contradiction of the shared rules that people publicly support and privately disregard. In her writing she probes the surface of genteel behavior to expose the indelicate, sometimes horrifying thoughts and actions that many would prefer to ignore; she does so with Rose and the fraudulent minister in "Wild Swans."

As a writer, Munro casts herself in the role of observer, the watcher and the thinker. It is the deep reflection and varying degrees of remove, as suggested by James Lynch's 1993 painting *Outside Looking In* (The Maas Gallery, London), that imbues her stories with their many depths and layers.

People in Munro's Fiction. Munro's major characters are usually female, whether children, adolescents, or adults. Many of her heroines rebel against custom; some, like Rose, are intensely curious. The women are often involved in dysfunctional relationships; they may be writers or artists; they may have children. Frequently Munro employs a female

SOME INSPIRATIONS BEHIND MUNRO'S WORK

The rural area of southwestern Ontario where Alice Munro grew up was a primary influence on her writing. Much of her work is set in small towns with vaguely familiar Scotch-Irish names such as Walley, Carstairs, and Hanratty. Her strong sense of place and love of landscape are revealed in sensory detail. Because she is so closely identified with this region, it has become known as "Alice Munro country."

Although some other stories are set in British Columbia, where she lived during her first marriage, Munro's heart is with the customs and speech of the country surrounding Lake Huron, and her best work seldom ventures beyond the borders of Ontario. Munro incorporated local history into "A Wilderness Story"—in the death of a Munro ancestor—and into "Meneseteung," which describes the life of an obscure Canadian poet.

Munro's family also provided important models for her more autobiographical stories, including the figures of the reserved father and two elderly aunts. The most significant model is her mother, who appears in various guises. This mother figure can be seen in determined, intense Ada Jordan in *Lives of Girls and Women*; in the awkward, ill mother of "Red Dress—1946" and "Friend of My Youth"; and in the shuffling and incoherent woman her daughters call Our Gothic Mother in "The Peace of Utrecht." This last story marks a turning point in Munro's career. It was, Munro said, the first story that she felt she had to write in order to exorcise her mother's ghost and her own sense of guilt.

Munro also acknowledges the early influence of Emily Brontë's *Wuthering Heights* and Margaret Mitchell's *Gone with the Wind* (1936), as well as the gothic writers of the American South, such as Carson McCullers, Eudora Welty, and Flannery O'Connor. All of these writers, notably, are women.

The bleak and rural landscape of Ontario often provides a fitting backdrop for the spiritual and emotional isolation with which many of Munro's characters wrangle. Together yet alone, much like Munro's protagonists, the figures in Hughie Lee-Smith's 1966 oil painting *Two Girls* (New Jersey State Museum) turn their back to the viewer, choosing to reveal nothing.

narrator, a device that might incorrectly suggest to some readers that the narrative voice is her own.

Munro's characters are mostly drawn from small-town and rural Canadian life: They are poor but proud Scotch-Irish farmers who can still recite the poems they memorized as schoolchildren, young seekers, various eccentrics, and redoubtable old ladies. Many are outsiders. Others are thoroughly unsympathetic, such as the self-centered ex-husband in "Lichen."

Themes in Munroe's Fiction. Munro's early work, with its eager young women, embraces themes of initiation and innocence lost. Several stories chart painful relationships or marriages, and few end happily. Her characters gradually come of age as their illusions about life are shattered. Even the more mature characters, such as the grandmother in "Save the Reaper," experience the chilling recognition of sinister forces present in their own neighborhoods lurking just beneath the smooth surface of things.

There is a gothic undercurrent in much of Munro's work, an unsettling mixture of the commonplace and the bizarre. While her earliest writing focuses on young women who are faced with ordinary difficulties, later stories contain gothic elements of mystery, horror, and even death or maiming. The collections *Open Secrets* and *The Love of a Good Woman* are particularly dark.

Writing Style. Munro penetrates the smooth surface of reality by means of her literary style. She employs a type of double vision to illustrate the complexities of her world. In an interview she once explained, "Mostly in my stories I like to look at what people don't understand.... What we think is happening and what we understand later on."

Munro utilizes a technique called layering to intensify this complexity. She admitted that she preferred a story to have several levels of meaning so that her reader can "think of something else" instead of concentrating on plot. Typically, more than one explanation for an event is possible. Such multiple possibilities may be seen in the stories "Carried Away" and "Open Secrets."

The growing complexity of Munro's work is also reinforced by abrupt time shifts, beginning with the stories in *Something I've Been Meaning to Tell You*. The trend to longer, structurally more complicated stories continues with her collections *The Moons of Jupiter: Stories* (1982) and *The Progress of Love* (1986). Demanding more of the reader, these later stories must often be read more than once, because the crucial elements are the things that are held back and not told. Munro has suggested that this holding back of information may be a Canadian trait. Thus, Del Jordan cringes at her mother's straightforwardness, which contrasts with the oblique irony common in her father's family.

BIBLIOGRAPHY

Blodgett, E. D. *Alice Munro*. Boston: Twayne Publishers, 1988.

Howells, Coral Ann. *Alice Munro*. Manchester, England: Manchester University Press, 1998.

MacKendrick, Louis K., ed. *Probable Fictions: Alice Munro's Narrative Acts*. Toronto: ECW Press, 1983.

Martin, W. R. *Alice Munro: Paradox and Parallel*. Edmonton: University of Alberta Press, 1987.

Miller, Judith, ed. *The Art of Alice Munro: Saying the Unsayable*. Waterloo, Ont.: University of Waterloo Press, 1984.

Miller, Lori. "I Know Where the Rope Is Attached." *The New York Times Book Review*, September 14, 1986, p. 7.

Munro, Alice. "What Is Real?" *Canadian Forum* 62 (September 1982): 5, 36.

Rasporich, Beverly J. *Dance of the Sexes: Art and Gender in the Fiction of Alice Munro*. Edmonton: University of Alberta Press, 1990.

Ross, Catherine Sheldrick. *Alice Munro: A Double Life*. Toronto: ECW Press, 1992.

Turbide, Diane. "The Incomparable Storyteller." *Maclean's* 107 (October 17, 1994): 46.

Reader's Guide to Major Works

LIVES OF GIRLS AND WOMEN

Genre: Novel
Subgenre: Coming-of-age story
Published: Toronto, 1971
Time period: 1940s and 1950s
Setting: Ontario, Canada

Themes and Issues. The scope of *Lives of Girls and Women* is limited to ten years in the life of Del Jordan, an adolescent girl living in Jubilee, Ontario, Alice Munro's fictionalized version of her hometown of Wingham. Recurring conflict can be seen in Del's resistance to her mother and her rejection of the many ways in which her community limits women's lives.

Munro said that she wrote a female version of the coming-of-age novel in order to explore a girl's awakening to experiences found, until then, only in stories about young men. In its final chapter, the book takes on a new dimension, shifting from a *Bildungsroman*, or a novel about building a life, to a *Künstlerroman*, a novel about the development of an artist. Del will become a writer, recording and interpreting what she learns.

The Plot. Del Jordan lives with her parents on a farm at the end of the Flats Road leading out of Jubilee. She is keenly aware of being poor and of not fitting in, perhaps because of her mother, Ada, who is better educated than most of their neighbors. During the school year Ada rents a house in town for herself and the two children, selling encyclopedias door to door to make ends meet. Ada loves knowledge but is still unaware of the dangers of being different. Del does understand this risk and keeps a low profile.

As Del matures, she investigates organized religion, which, as her mother did, she will eventually reject. In a disturbing chapter, her sexual curiosity is exploited by Mr. Chamberlain, a friend of the family's boarder. From this episode, Del learns that she desires the same freedom that men have to discard unwanted experiences and to reject the shame that somehow adheres only to women.

Unlike her friend Naomi, Del scorns the sex roles endorsed by her neighbors. She rejects a

In Helen Lundeberg's 1935 painting *Double Portrait of the Artist in Time* (National Museum of American Art, Washington, D.C.), the experiences of the little girl cast long shadows that stretch far into the life of the adult. In Munro's *Lives of Girls and Women*, the story of Del's youth and coming-of-age eventually transcends itself, becoming fused with and inseparable from the arc of her development as an artist.

ALICE MUNRO   1079

famous psychiatrist's distinction between male and female thought processes: As a boy and girl sit on a park bench looking at the moon, the boy marvels at the universe, while the girl decides to wash her hair. Defiantly, Del prepares for her university entrance exams until she meets a young laborer, Garnet French, at a revival meeting. Their attraction to each other is clearly physical; it has nothing to do with ideas.

In an awkward sexual episode, Del is initiated into womanhood. Garnet wants to marry her but insists that she first must be baptized by total immersion. While they are swimming, he tries to force her to agree and nearly drowns her. Fighting for her life, Del finally claims her own power. By this crucial act she defines herself—not through sex or religion but through her own independence.

In the final chapter, Del begins to write an amateurish gothic romance based on the story of a local family. She soon abandons the fanciful story for real questions and real life, just as she has abandoned her fantasy of Garnet French. She realizes that people's lives are a mixture of dreams and necessary reality, "deep caves paved with kitchen linoleum."

Analysis. *Lives of Girls and Women* offers the experience of an adolescent girl with the insights of an adult. Del is eager and curious; she develops independence and daring. As she matures, she becomes more aware of the inconsistencies in her world. As an evolving writer, she learns to evaluate different perceptions of reality and to choose one for herself.

Although Munro published a disclaimer that her novel is not autobiographical "in fact" and that its characters are not modeled on real people, reaction in her home town of Wingham was disapproving. A decade after its publication, a local newspaper editorial still complained that residents had been attacked and insulted by her depictions of them. That initial reaction was muted, however, when, in 1991, Munro was honored with the Canadian Council Molson Prize for the Arts for her "outstanding contribution to the cultural and intellectual life of Canada."

SOURCES FOR FURTHER STUDY

Besner, Neil. *Introducing Alice Munro's "Lives of Girls and Women": A Reader's Guide.* Toronto: ECW Press, 1990.

Blodgett, E. D. *Alice Munro.* Boston: Twayne Publishers, 1988.

Martin, W. R. *Alice Munro Paradox and Parallel.* Edmonton: University of Alberta Press, 1987.

WHO DO YOU THINK YOU ARE?
Genre: Short stories
Subgenre: Coming-of-age stories

SHORT FICTION
- 1968 Dance of the Happy Shades
- 1974 Something I've Been Meaning to Tell You: Thirteen Stories
- 1978 Who Do You Think You Are? (pb. in U.S. as The Beggar Maid: Stories of Flo and Rose, 1979)
- 1982 The Moons of Jupiter: Stories
- 1986 The Progress of Love
- 1990 Friend of My Youth: Stories
- 1994 Open Secrets: Stories
- 1996 Selected Stories
- 1998 The Love of a Good Woman: Stories

LONG FICTION
- 1971 Lives of Girls and Women

Published: Toronto, 1978
Time period: 1930s to 1970s
Setting: Ontario and British Columbia, Canada

Themes and Issues. This collection, published in the United States as *The Beggar Maid: Stories of Flo and Rose* in 1979, contains ten linked but discontinuous stories in the life of Rose, a girl who grows into womanhood. In Hanratty, the small town where her stepmother, Flo, owns a store, Rose is initiated into the mysteries of class, sexuality, and social behavior. Later, Rose will challenge the larger society and its concept of what a woman's life should be.

The Plot. Although *Who Do You Think You Are?* contains separate episodes, together they are coherent enough to form a recognizable plot. Rose's childhood is troubling. She attends a two-room school where cruel children run rampant and the teacher cowers in the classroom. At home Rose taunts her stepmother until Flo is forced to call upon Rose's father for discipline. He beats Rose with a belt, a repeated ritual that seems to satisfy everyone. Rose maintains a love-hate relationship with Flo, the only mother she has ever known, and a part of her thrills to the wild, gossipy stories Flo reveals about their neighbors.

When a teenage Rose takes the train alone to Toronto, Flo cautions her against speaking to "white slavers" who may pose as ministers and try to kidnap her. Predictably, Rose ignores Flo's warnings. After a man sitting next to her introduces himself as a minister and covertly touches her knee, Rose cannot tell him to stop.

Munro's fiction often focuses on the deep gulf, the distances and irreconcilable differences, that exists between mothers and daughters. This emotional separation is eloquently captured in Dorothea Lange's 1939 photograph *Child and Her Mother, Wapato, Yakima Valley, Washington* (Oakland Museum of California).

She is overwhelmed by curiosity and a need to know—despite the consequences.

Once she enters university, Rose becomes uncomfortably aware that she is poor. She works at the library, where she meets Patrick, a graduate student from a wealthy family. Patrick, a romantic, believes he is rescuing a damsel in distress, for Rose reminds him of Sir Edward Burne-Jones's Victorian painting *King Cophetua and the Beggar Maid* (1884). Patrick determines to marry and remake Rose, for which kindness, he believes, she will be eternally grateful. Unfortunately, the marriage is a disaster. Patrick is very conventional; Rose is a rebel. After ten years the couple divorces, and Rose embarks on a series of casual affairs.

Purely by chance, Rose becomes an actress when she meets a man who is seeking someone with a country accent for his play. After her divorce Rose works at a small radio station and then teaches drama in upstate Ontario. Later, she finds a job acting in a television series filmed in Vancouver.

Rose finally returns to Hanratty to visit Flo, who now lives alone, but she finds that her stepmother seems confused and has difficulty getting around. She realizes that Flo can no longer take care of herself and regretfully places her in the county home. Rose finally acknowledges Flo's importance to her, even as the old woman sinks into senility.

Analysis. Rose is quite different from Del Jordan, with whom she is often compared. Like Del, Rose has experiences from which she learns, but she is less focused. Her broader history takes her from early childhood through marriage, motherhood, and divorce to middle age. Rose is not a particularly admirable character, but she is a survivor, and she can see herself with some clarity by the book's end.

The book's two titles offer a dual interpretation. The Canadian title, *Who Do You Think You Are?*, repeats a mocking phrase directed at Rose, who is calling attention to herself, but it also echoes her determined search for an adult identity. Curious Rose is anxious to find out what will happen to her, but she does not know who she is for a long time. Munro's American publisher changed the book's title to *The Beggar Maid*, which suggests Patrick's idealized view of Rose and his inability to recognize the real woman she is. Like *Lives of Girls and Women*, this book received the Governor-General's Literary Award.

SOURCES FOR FURTHER STUDY

Fowler, Rowena. "The Art of Alice Munro: *The Beggar Maid* and *Lives of Girls and Women*." *Critique: Studies in Modern Fiction* 25 (Summer 1984): 189–198.

Howells, Coral Ann. *Alice Munro*. Manchester, England: Manchester University Press, 1998.

Hoy, Helen. "'Dull, Simple, Amazing, and Unfathomable': Paradox and Double Vision in Alice Munro's Fiction." *Studies in Canadian Literature* 5 (Spring 1980): 100–115.

Other Works

"BOYS AND GIRLS" (1968). A widely anthologized story, "Boys and Girls" is set on a fox farm near the fictional town of Jubilee, Ontario. A young girl dreams of heroic deeds as she does chores with her father, with whom she identifies. When he shoots an old workhorse for meat to feed the foxes, she bravely watches.

From her visiting grandmother, the girl hears of the rules set by the outside world: Girls do not slam doors; girls sit with their knees together; girls mind their proper business. Her illusions under attack, she begins to realize that, as a girl, she will be excluded from many areas of experience. Identification with her father is not allowed; in reality, she is expected to help her mother with women's work, while her little brother will take her coveted place beside her father.

In many Munro stories, such as "Boys and Girls," women are compromised and often trapped by the inflexible and short-sighted roles in which society casts them. In Hughie Lee-Smith's 1958 oil painting *Impedimenta*, these obstacles and limitations materialize in the form of a divisive coil barring communication and exchange. Brooding and disheartened, the young woman is forced to turn within.

When her father and his hired man decide to slaughter Flora, a spirited mare, to feed the foxes, the girl suddenly rebels. Although she is ordered to shut the gate and trap the mare, she deliberately leaves the gate open so that Flora can gallop away. After the men chase and capture Flora, the girl's brother reveals what she has done. "Never mind," her father says dismissively, "she's only a girl." Her disillusion is complete.

"THE PEACE OF UTRECHT" (1968). This story, occasioned by the death of Munro's mother, explores anguished mother-daughter relationships. After ten years, Helen visits her sister Maddy in Jubilee. Years before, when Helen left for college and marriage, Maddy stayed behind to care for their sick mother, who had Parkinson's disease. During the previous winter the mother died, but Helen did not return for the funeral. Now she has come to make peace with the dead. In her bedroom, she finds her high school history notes on the eighteenth-century Peace of Utrecht, which ended the War of the Spanish Succession. The pages of her notes are like the fragments of knowledge that she is piecing together.

Helen recalls how she and Maddy resented their mother, refusing to see her as anything but a burden. She remembers the humiliation she endured because of her mother's slurred speech and her rolling eyes. Overcome with remorse, Helen now recognizes that her mother was a prisoner of her disease, unable to walk, talk, or care for herself, dependent on two daughters who longed only to get away from her.

Helen visits her elderly aunts, who confide that Maddy finally put her mother in the hospital, where no one could understand her speech. Even when the mother, who was growing progressively worse, begged to come home, Maddy refused. One aunt reports how the mother fled the hospital at night, only to be caught. The nurses nailed a board across her bed so she could not escape again. Within two months the mother was dead. Maddy cannot acknowledge her feelings of guilt; yet now that she is free of her mother, she cannot leave Jubilee. Ironically, she, too, is trapped.

"SOMETHING I'VE BEEN MEANING TO TELL YOU" (1974). The title story of Munro's second collection, "Something I've Been Meaning to Tell You" offers an example of the gothic elements recurrent throughout Munro's work. Et Desmond, a self-reliant and successful dressmaker, remains close to her beautiful older sister, Char, and Char's pleasant husband, Arthur, a high school history teacher. Char and Arthur are forced to cancel their vacation in Yellowstone Park because of his sudden illness. Soon afterward, the still-charming Blaikie Noble returns to town to work as a tour guide for the local resort hotel once owned by his family.

Nearly forty years before, Char had a youthful romance with Blaikie Noble, that ended when he eloped with a hotel guest. Et has always seen through Noble and has been unimpressed. Et, who enjoys coddling Arthur, offers to fix him something to eat and discovers a container of rat poison in the kitchen cupboard. A practical woman, she dislikes mysteries. She begins to worry about the poison, Arthur's health, and even Char, who seems more distant than ever.

Munro uses a complex series of time shifts to unfold this account of secret passion and death lurking beneath a genteel facade. The characters are not who they appear to be, and beneath their proper exteriors lies an undreamed-of intensity. This strange and subtle story ends in uncertainty and surprise, leaving the reader to wonder which possible reality to accept.

Resources

A major collection of Alice Munro's papers, including correspondence, notebooks, manuscript drafts, essays, and articles, is held in the Special Collection at the MacKimmie Library of the University of Calgary, Alberta. Archival material gathered by Dr. Walter R. Martin for his study *Alice Munro: Parallel and Paradox* (1987) has been donated to the library of the University of Waterloo, Ontario. It includes manuscripts as well as biographical and critical articles on Munro and may also be referenced on the Web. (http://www.lib.uwaterloo.ca/discipline/SpecColl/archives/munmart.html)

Many critical references appear in Canadian publications that are not widely available in the United States. Several are quoted in reference works such as *Contemporary Literary Criticism* and *Book Review Digest*. Other sources of interest for students of Alice Munro include the following:

Alice Munro Biocritical Essay. In Thomas E. Tausky's 1986 essay, included in the Alice Munro Papers at the University of Calgary, he excerpts earlier interviews with Munro, including one of his own, and discusses the composition of her work from a chronological perspective. His essay may be found on a separate Web site. (http://www.ucalgary.ca/library/SpecColl/munrobioc.htm).

Online Reading Guides. The Random House Web site hosts reading guides for Munro's *Open Secrets* and *The Love of a Good Woman*, including questions, discussion topics, and author biographies, to enhance group or individual reading. (http://www.randomhouse.com/catalog/display)

Video Recordings. Several of Munro's stories have been filmed and are available on video, including *Connection* (1986), *Lives of Girls and Women* (1994), and *The Ottawa Valley* (1974).

JOANNE MCCARTHY

Frank Norris

BORN: March 5, 1870, Chicago, Illinois
DIED: October 25, 1902, San Francisco, California
IDENTIFICATION: One of North America's most notable naturalistic novelists, Frank Norris is remembered for his commentaries on how big business exploits and cheats common people, particularly farmers.

Although he lived only thirty-two years, Frank Norris produced an important body of writing. Noted for two novels dealing with growing and distributing wheat, *The Octopus* (1901) and *The Pit* (1903), Norris, in his novel *McTeague* (1899), also wrote one of the most memorable studies of human failure ever published. Norris, influenced by the French writer Émile Zola's naturalism, marks a turning point in American literature's evolution from the genteel traditionalism of realists such as William Dean Howells, Henry James, and Hamlin Garland to the socially conscious naturalism of Stephen Crane, Theodore Dreiser, and Upton Sinclair. Norris's influence upon authors such as William Faulkner, John Steinbeck, and Ernest Hemingway is undeniable.

The Writer's Life

Frank Norris squeezed a great deal of experience into his short life, and he saw five of his novels published before his death at thirty-two. Several additional volumes were published posthumously.

The Early Years. Frank Norris was born Benjamin Franklin Norris, Jr., the son of Benjamin Franklin Norris and Gertrude Doggett Norris. His father was head of a wholesale jewelry company in Chicago. From humble beginnings, Benjamin Norris advanced much like the characters in the then-popular stories by Horatio Alger that depicted worthy young men who strike out on their own and succeed through hard work and dedication.

Gertrude Norris, who had left teaching for a career on the stage, provided the family's main cultural influence. After her marriage she devoted herself to her family, but she continued to indulge her flair for the dramatic by reading to Norris and his two brothers, Lester and Charles, from the novels of Sir Walter Scott and Charles Dickens.

In 1882 the Norrises, now affluent, bought a mansion on Chicago's Michigan Avenue. In 1884, however, Chicago's harsh winters drove them west to Oakland, California. The following year, the elder Benjamin bought a ten-thousand-dollar home on Sacramento Street in San Francisco, which was at that time one of the city's most expensive houses.

Benjamin, Sr., became rich building houses and selling them at twice their construction cost. A pillar of the community, he taught Sunday school classes and was a leader in the Browning Society, a literary group. The Gilded Age in which Norris grew up was characterized by social stratification, conspicuous consumption, and a quest for culture. Norris, a product of this age, became one of its staunchest critics.

Education. Norris was an undisciplined student. He persevered in subjects that interested him but totally dismissed those that did not. He shunned the college preparatory cur-

Norris's childhood years were marked by luxury and indulgence. Though they offered him a life of ease, it was still a legacy with which he grew increasingly uncomfortable. It clashed with his own romantic notions of the self-made man, the writer of the people.

Norris is pictured here, gloves in his hand and dog at his feet, in the center of his fraternity brothers at the University of California in this 1893 photograph. The budding writer took instantly to the diverse, vibrant community of peers.

riculum of the private school he attended in Belmont, California, and spent most of his time there playing with toy soldiers and composing stories about them. He left this school after he broke his arm playing football, and his father, eager to prepare Norris for life, enrolled him in San Francisco's Boys' High School. However, Norris rebelled against its traditional curriculum and, with his mother's blessing, left to study painting at the San Francisco Art Association.

Norris demonstrated some natural artistic ability, and his parents decided that their son, now seventeen, should study painting abroad. Originally Benjamin was to accompany him while Gertrude remained in San Francisco with Lester and Charles. In June 1887, however, Lester died of diphtheria at age nine. The remaining Norrises then journeyed abroad. When Frank found that London did not offer the training he wanted, the family went with him to Paris, where he continued his studies at the Atelier Julien.

Norris then persuaded his mother to accompany him to Italy so he could study painting in Rome and Florence. When his interest waned, he studied fencing and regularly attended the Italian opera. After reading an English translation of the medieval writer Jean Froissart's *Chronicles* (1523–1525), he developed an enthusiastic interest in medieval armor.

College Years. Norris's family returned to San Francisco in 1888, leaving him alone in

Europe. In 1889, unhappy with his painting and his father's goading, he returned home to enter the University of California at Berkeley with limited status. At Berkeley, he studied English and continued his writing. He joined the Phi Gamma Sigma fraternity, which influenced him profoundly.

Four years at Berkeley resulted neither in his gaining regular status nor in his receiving a degree. He felt overwhelmed by his classes, but his fraternity provided him with a refuge. During his second year at Berkeley, Norris completed his long ballad *Yvernelle: A Tale of Feudal France* (1892), and his mother subsidized its publication.

In 1894 Norris's parents were divorced. Benjamin soon remarried, and when he died in 1900, he bequeathed his entire million-dollar estate to his second wife. Norris appeared to be unaffected by his father's death and unconcerned about the distribution of his estate.

Upon receiving her divorce decree, Gertrude moved with her sons to Boston, Massachusetts. There Norris entered Harvard University as a special student and studied writing with Lewis E. Gates, who became a substantial force in his creative life. He studied French and read much of Émile Zola, France's most notable naturalistic novelist.

After College. By 1895 Norris was weary of university life and craved adventure. With a commitment to write about his adventures for the San Francisco *Chronicle*, he set out for Cape Town, South Africa. He planned a leisurely overland trip to Cairo, sending the *Chronicle* reports en route. His plans went awry, however, when he developed a nagging fever. When he recovered, the Transvaal, then immersed in conflict between the Boers and the British, expelled him. Norris returned home physically weakened.

Within six weeks, Norris regained his strength and took a job with *The Wave*, a newspaper created to publicize the Del Monte Hotel on the Monterey Peninsula of

William Hahn's 1875 oil painting *Harvest Time* (Fine Arts Museum of San Francisco) captures the yearly bustle that clutched the San Joaquin Valley. In *The Octopus*, Norris wrote, "The wheat, now close to its maturity, had turned from pale yellow to golden yellow, and from that to brown. Like a gigantic carpet, it spread itself over all the land. There was nothing else to be seen but the limitless sea of wheat as far as the eye could reach, dry, rustling, crisp and harsh in the rare breaths of hot wind out of the southeast."

HIGHLIGHTS IN NORRIS'S LIFE

1870 Benjamin Franklin Norris, Jr., is born in Chicago, Illinois.
1878 Tours Europe with family; brother Lester is born.
1881 Brother Charles is born.
1882 Family moves to mansion on Chicago's Michigan Avenue.
1884 Family moves to Oakland, California.
1885 Family resettles in San Francisco, California.
1886 Norris studies at Boys' High School, then at the San Francisco Art Association.
1887 Studies art in England, France, and Italy.
1889 Abandons studies and returns to San Francisco; publishes first article in the San Francisco *Chronicle*.
1889 Enters the University of California at Berkeley.
1892 Publishes long ballad *Yvernelle: A Tale of Feudal France*; joins Phi Gamma Delta fraternity.
1894 Parents divorce; Norris moves to Boston with mother and brother; enters Harvard University.
1895 Goes to South Africa as correspondent for the *Chronicle*.
1896 Develops persistent fever; is expelled from the Transvaal; joins staff of *The Wave*; meets Jeannette Black.
1898 Publishes *Moran of the Lady Letty*; works at Doubleday and McClure; goes to Cuba to report on Spanish-American War for *McClure's*; contracts malaria.
1899 Publishes *McTeague* and *Blix*.
1900 Marries Jeannette Black; publishes *A Man's Woman*; completes *The Octopus*.
1901 Goes to Chicago to gather material for *The Pit*.
1902 Daughter, Jeannette, Jr., is born; Norrises move to San Francisco; wife has appendectomy; Norris dies of perforated appendix and peritonitis on October 25

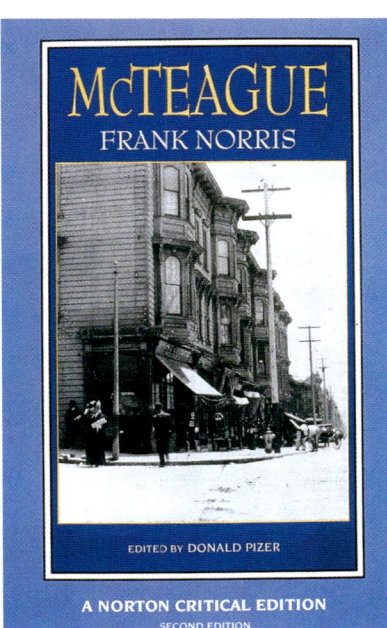

FILMS BASED ON NORRIS'S STORIES

1909	A Corner in Wheat
1914	Desert Gold
1914	The Pit
1916	Life's Whirlpool
1922	Moran of the Lady Letty
1924	Greed

California. In two years, Norris wrote over one hundred pieces for *The Wave*. He earned little but lived a comfortable life through his mother's generosity. During much of this period, however, he was discouraged and became cynical.

In 1896 Norris met Jeannette Black, then seventeen, who served as the inspiration for *Moran of the Lady Letty*, which was serialized in *The Wave* in 1898. Early that year, Norris went to New York to work at Doubleday and McClure as an editorial assistant. In New York, Norris became friendly with the author-poet Hamlin Garland as well as William Dean Howells, the most celebrated man of American letters at that time.

Norris's employer, S. S. McClure, published *McClure's* magazine, for which Norris sailed to Cuba as a Spanish-American War correspondent in April 1898. During the trip he met Stephen Crane, whose work he respected but with whom he shared little common ground, and Richard Harding Davis, of whom he was too much in awe to form a close relationship. His trip ended when he contracted malaria.

When he married Jeannette Black in January 1900, Norris was a manuscript reader at Doubleday, Page and Company. After reading Theodore Dreiser's manuscript *Sister Carrie* (1900)—the story of an ambitious young girl's rise from poverty to affluence—he praised it so enthusiastically that Doubleday offered Dreiser a contract. However, upon realizing how controversial it was, Doubleday attempted to withdraw the contract. Dreiser and Norris both stood firm, and the novel, which greatly inspired Norris, appeared amid relentless public outcry.

Norris had returned to California for two months in 1899 to gather material for the first of his projected three novels on growing and distributing wheat. In 1900 he completed the first of these three novels, *The Octopus*, and it was published the following April. The Norrises then went briefly to Chicago, where Norris gathered information for *The Pit*, his second novel about wheat.

Norris and his wife returned from Chicago to California, where in February 1902, Jeannette gave birth to a daughter, Jeannette, Jr. Norris finished *The Pit* and planned an around-the-world boat trip with his wife and daughter. In October, Jeannette had an appendectomy, and in caring for her, Norris neglected his own symptoms of appendicitis. On October 25, 1902, he died of a perforated appendix and peritonitis. "The Wolf," which was to be the third novel of his proposed trilogy, remained unwritten.

Following Norris's death, his brother, Charles Gilman Norris, himself a novelist and the husband of the novelist Kathleen Norris, published *Vandover and the Brute* (1914) with some of his own additions. In 1928 Charles Gilman Norris edited a number of his brother's miscellaneous works for the tenth volume of *The Complete Edition of Frank Norris*, and in 1931 he helped Oscar Lewis with the production of *Frank Norris of "The Wave."*

The Writer's Work

Many think that Frank Norris, as a writer, was responding to two opposing forces in his life. His father wanted him to be practical and to accomplish something materially significant. His mother envisioned him as an artist. In achieving literary success with his novels, Norris sought, at least subconsciously, to please both of his parents.

Major Issues. Norris planned two epic trilogies: one on the growth and distribution of wheat and the other on the three days of the Civil War Battle of Gettysburg. At the time of his death in 1902, only the first novel in the wheat trilogy, *The Octopus*, had been published. It described the planting and harvesting of wheat in California's San Joaquin Valley. The trilogy's second part, *The Pit*, was published posthumously in 1903 and followed the wheat as it was processed and sold through Chicago's grain market. The proposed third novel of Norris's wheat trilogy, "The Wolf," was to focus on the international distribution of wheat. Norris had outlined parts of "The Wolf" before his death but had not yet begun any work on the Gettysburg trilogy.

In *The Octopus* and *The Pit*, Norris writes about the exploitation of ranchers, who are dependent upon the railroads to get their produce to market and upon Chicago traders to sell it. Norris, however, does not wholly condemn the businessmen who often took advantage of the ranchers. Although he clearly respects the ranchers, he also has an undeni-

Norris's use of the octopus, in the novel of the same name, as a symbol of the railroad is rich with diverse connotations. Through their powerful influence, the rail companies were able to reach out and grab land for their own use. At the same time, the tracks themselves, suggested here in Stan Backus's 1939 watercolor *Santa Margarita Grade* (Los Angeles County Museum of Art), were like long tentacled arms, sticking to the land and stretching out in all directions.

SOME INSPIRATIONS BEHIND NORIS'S WORK

Frank Norris's earliest literary influences came from his mother, who read to her children from the novels of Sir Walter Scott and Charles Dickens. While Norris studied art in Europe, he became familiar with librettos of Italian opera, and his novels often reflect a similar mix of melodrama, romanticism, and naturalism. In Europe, he read the *Chronicles* of Jean Froissart, which inspired his interest in medieval armor.

During Norris's year at Harvard University, he was greatly inspired by his writing teacher, Lewis E. Gates. At Harvard he read books that directly influenced his own writing, including a great deal of George Eliot. He was particularly inspired by the naturalism of Émile Zola, the most celebrated naturalist writer of that era. He read Stephen Crane's *Maggie: A Girl of the Streets* (1893) and admired Crane's choice of a fallen woman, a common girl with a brutish father and a mother too much concerned with public opinion, as the book's protagonist. His reading of Charles Darwin's *On the Origin of Species by Means of Natural Selection* (1859) influenced Norris profoundly and reinforced his naturalistic views. Darwin's theory of evolution led Norris to conclude that human actions and development lie essentially outside human control.

At work in the publishing world of New York, Norris had the opportunity to meet many authors, of whom the most influential were Theodore Dreiser, Richard Harding Davis, and William Dean Howells.

Norris's wife, Jeannette Black, was reputedly the inspiration for the title character in his first novel, *Moran of the Lady Letty*.

able admiration for those who have created the complex structure underlying worldwide trade in commodities.

Norris questions the growth and distribution structure as a whole, finding many of its elements corrupt and destructive. However, while some of the business dealings he describes may be treacherous, they lead to a good general outcome. This is surely a romantic view of life. Naturalism is concerned with determinism, which emphasizes the inability of humans to control the forces that shape them.

These forces grind on relentlessly, crushing whatever stands in their way. One must adapt or be crushed. Norris believed that naturalism is more closely related to romanticism than to realism.

Demonstrating this contention is Vanamee in *The Octopus*. Vanamee's fiancé, Angelé Varian, who has been made pregnant during a rape, dies in childbirth. Years later, Vanamee encounters Angelé's grown child and discovers that she is a virtual duplicate of her dead mother. Vanamee is comforted by knowing the girl. Although Angelé's child is produced by a vicious act, the end result is good.

As the United States moved rapidly from an agricultural to an industrial economy, Norris depicted the conflicts that accompany such a shift. He focused on the pressures brought about by the new industrialism and how they affected his characters. The intrinsic integrity of his ranchers, such as Magnus Derrick and his son Lyman, is continually tested, as they are forced to compromise their ideals to achieve their own goals.

Norris's Characters. Among Norris's best-remembered characters is McTeague, the hapless, unlicensed dentist who moves unceasingly toward his own destruction never quite perceiving his fate or how to avoid it. McTeague's wife, Trina, demonstrates the corruptive power of money. *McTeague* is essentially about human greed and its consequences, as exemplified in two tragic characters, Zerkow, the junk dealer, and McTeague, both of whom emphasize Norris's themes of indulgence and retribution.

In his long poem *Yvernelle*, Norris makes clear his notion that evil is inherited but virtue is acquired. In his early apprenticeship work, *Vandover and the Brute*, written during his year at Harvard, he condemns self-indulgence, perhaps ruminating on his own indulgences during his formative years.

Despite the severe flaws in Norris's first published novel, *Moran of the Lady Letty*, one notes the same philosophy that pervades *McTeague* and *The Octopus*. Moran, the novel's shipwrecked protagonist, says, "The strongest of us are going to live, the weakest are going to die. I'm going to live and I'm going to have my loot, too." Here one finds a clear statement of Charles Darwin's theory of the survival of the fittest.

The evils that concern Norris—greed, blind ambition, dishonesty—are not unlike the religious concept of original sin. Norris's most memorable characters—notably McTeague, Trina, Zerkow, Magnus and Lyman Derrick, and Curtis Jadwin—are driven by evil forces deep within them. Each suffers the punishment that accompanies such evil. Nevertheless, Norris remained convinced that, in time, evil generates good. It could be argued that one of Norris's major strengths is his ability to sensitively portray characters of questionable moral values. In his significantly flawed novel *A Man's Woman* (1900), he presents with a degree of sympathy and understanding the two central and offensive characters, Ward Bennett and Lloyd Searight.

BIBLIOGRAPHY

Boyd, Jennifer. *Frank Norris: Spatial Form and Narrative Time*. New York: Peter Lang, 1993.

Buss, David M. *The Evolution of Desire*. New York: HarperCollins, 1994.

Campbell, Donna M. *Resisting Regionalism: Gender and Naturalism in American Fiction, 1885–1915*. Athens: Ohio University Press, 1997.

Civello, Paul. *American Literary Naturalism and Its Twentieth-Century Transformations*. Athens: University of Georgia Press, 1994.

French, Warren. *Frank Norris*. New York: Twayne Publishers, 1962.

Hochman, Barbara. *The Art of Frank Norris, Storyteller*. New York: Columbia University Press, 1988.

Hussman, Lawrence E. *Harbingers of a Century: The Novels of Frank Norris*. New York: Peter Lang, 1999.

McElrath, Joseph R., Jr. *Frank Norris Revisited*. New York: Twayne Publishers, 1992.

Myers, Eric. "Mining *McTeague*'s Gold." *New York Times Magazine*, October 25, 1992, 46.

Pizer, Donald. *The Novels of Frank Norris*. Bloomington: Indiana University Press, 1966.

Reader's Guide to Major Works

MCTEAGUE
Genre: Novel
Subgenre: Naturalistic
Published: New York, 1899
Time period: Late nineteenth century
Setting: San Francisco and Death Valley, California

Themes and Issues. Frank Norris did not give the self-named protagonist of *McTeague* a first name. Throughout the book this bungling, unlicensed, dim-witted San Francisco dentist is known simply as McTeague. He is a daring choice for a protagonist: an unattractive, brutish, boring person. He is presented in such a way as to evoke interest but not sympathy. *McTeague* is a study in deception and greed and how these flaws bring out the downfall of its protagonist.

Norris is concerned with exploring McTeague's heredity as well as the environmental factors that have shaped him. McTeague is a miner who learns a little of the dental profession from a traveling dentist. Spurred by his mother's ambitions for him, he establishes an office on San Francisco's Polk Street and fraudulently passes himself off as a dentist.

Gripped by an uncontrollable lust that seems to originate somewhere outside of him, McTeague, portrayed by the actor Gibson Gowland in *Greed*, the silent film version of *McTeague*, leers at the etherized Trina, played by the actress Zasu Pitts.

McTeague—lacking in ambition, stupid, coarse, vulgar, and slothful—has established a safe haven for himself in his dental parlors. He relates to but generally remains detached from the life outside his windows. He takes pride in the large gold tooth that he has bought to hang outside his establishment. He also values his canary, which he keeps in a gilded cage. Throughout the novel, gold is a symbol for crass materialism.

The Plot. McTeague's boring life is relatively serene until Marcus Schouler enters it and becomes his best friend. Marcus is considerably more sophisticated than McTeague and can discuss political matters that are beyond McTeague's comprehension. He brings his cousin, Trina Sieppe, whom he has considered marrying, to McTeague's office to have a tooth repaired.

McTeague is smitten by Trina; while she is under anesthetic, he fondles and kisses her. Marcus, upon hearing that McTeague is interested in Trina, renounces his claim to her. McTeague proposes marriage, and Trina accepts. However, he soon discovers the dark side of Trina's personality when she wins five thousand dollars in a lottery. After she receives this windfall, she becomes miserly, eventually withdrawing her winnings in twenty-dollar gold coins from the bank in which she first deposited them.

Meanwhile, Marcus Schouler has revealed to the authorities the fact that McTeague has been practicing dentistry without a license. As a result, McTeague's dental parlors are shut down, leaving McTeague without means of support. After he fails at several menial jobs he finally appeals to Trina for help, but she refuses. They have a violent encounter in which McTeague bites Trina's hand so deeply that she loses it. Later, as she lies naked on her money, McTeague breaks in, murders her, takes her money, and flees.

LONG FICTION

- 1898 Moran of the Lady Letty
- 1899 McTeague
- 1899 Blix
- 1900 A Man's Woman
- 1901 The Octopus
- 1903 The Pit
- 1914 Vandover and the Brute

SHORT FICTION

- 1903 A Deal in Wheat and Other Stories of the New and Old West
- 1906 The Joyous Miracle
- 1909 The Third Circle
- 1931 Frank Norris of "The Wave," ed. Oscar Lewis

NONFICTION

- 1903 The Responsibilities of the Novelist
- 1917 The Surrender of Santiago
- 1956 The Letters of Frank Norris, ed. Franklin D. Walker
- 1964 The Literary Criticism of Frank Norris, ed. Donald Pizer

MISCELLANEOUS

- 1899 Complete Works
- 1903 The Golden Gate Edition of Frank Norris
- 1928 The Complete Edition of Frank Norris
- 1970 A Novelist in the Making: A Collection of Student Themes and the Novels of "Blix" and "Vandover and the Brute," ed. James D. Hart

POETRY

- 1892 Yvernelle: A Tale of Feudal France
- 1930 Two Poems and "Kim" Reviewed

McTeague, carrying his canary in its gilded cage, is pursued by Schouler into the desert near Death Valley. The two men fight. Schouler fires a shot that pierces McTeague's canteen, leaving him without water. McTeague fires a retaliatory shot, mortally injuring Schouler. Before Schouler dies, he handcuffs himself to McTeague, fatally linking the two in the desert.

Analysis. *McTeague* has major structural flaws, but it makes exceptionally successful use of sensory detail. Norris's powers of observation are at their best in parts of this novel. Although his use of symbolism is often heavy-handed, his subplots are effective.

Particularly successful is the subplot involving two elderly people who live in a boardinghouse, Old Grannis and Miss Baker. Each is too shy to let the other one know of a wish to communicate, but eventually the two form a bond. Supporting this subplot is one of two dogs separated by a wooden fence. They bark and growl at each other. When they finally meet, however, they back off.

Another subplot involves Zerkow, a greedy junk dealer who marries Maria Macapa, a demented charwoman who tells tales about a solid gold dinner set owned by her Guatemalan family. Zerkow dreams of having her lead him to this treasure so that he can snatch it. When she fails to do so, her slits her throat.

McTeague was shocking in its depiction of the greed and brutality of American life. It clearly challenged the genteel traditionalism that had characterized American literature of the preceding century, and it moved decidedly toward an emerging naturalism that would come to dominate the writing of the early twentieth century.

In this scene from *Greed,* McTeague and Marcus Schouler, portrayed by the actor Jean Hersholt, are about to become fatally bound in the desert. In this single image, Norris achieved the ideal marriage of swelling Romanticism and bleak naturalism.

SOURCES FOR FURTHER STUDY

Campbell, Donna M. *Resisting Regionalism: Gender and Naturalism in American Fiction, 1885–1915.* Athens: Ohio University Press, 1997.

French, Warren. *Frank Norris.* New York: Twayne Publishers, 1962.

Hussman, Lawrence E. *Harbingers of a Century: The Novels of Frank Norris.* New York: Peter Lang, 1999.

Wead, George. "Frank Norris: His Share of *Greed.*" In *The Classic American Novel and the Movies,* edited by Gerald Peary and Roger Shatzkin. New York: Frederick Ungar, 1977.

THE OCTOPUS

Genre: Novel
Subgenre: Naturalism
Published: New York, 1901
Time period: Late nineteenth century
Setting: San Francisco and San Joaquin Valley, California

Themes and Issues. The character of Presley in *The Octopus* serves as Norris's mouthpiece, often reflecting the author's own attitudes and philosophy. Presley looks out over the vast wheat fields of California's fertile San Joaquin Valley and wants to write an epic about wheat and the people who grow it. Norris set out to write just such an epic when he planned his three novels on the growth and distribution of wheat.

Like the ancient Trojans in Homer's *Iliad* (ca. 800 b.c.e.), the ranchers about whom Norris writes have endured a decade of unresolved conflict. Their antagonist, the Pacific and Southwest Railroad, is the looming symbolic octopus from which Norris's novel derives its title. Like an octopus, the railroad has a huge head—its administrative structure—as well as grasping appendages that can reach out and grab anything it wants.

Trains become nightmares for the hard-working ranchers who are dependent upon the railroad to haul their produce to market. Locomotives rumble across the countryside, their headlights like the eyes of a great Cyclops, shattering the tranquillity of the ranchers' valley. The intrusion is a constant reminder of the unfairness with which the railroad grasps land for its right-of-way, dictating its own terms, always to the disadvantage of the ill-fated ranchers, who cannot survive without the railroad but whose existence is threatened by its unfair practices.

Norris creates a conflict in which the individual ranchers are locked in combat against the railroad, personified by the vile railway agent S. Behrman and his unscrupulous henchmen. S. Behrman's lack of a first name

In *The Octopus*, Norris's critique of the gluttonous power of the railroads was based on historical fact. In this political cartoon from the late twentieth century, Thomas Nast skewers an industry often marked by questionable business practices. Freight rates were not always the same for everyone. The Erie and the New York Central, for example, entered into a trust agreement with the monopolistic conglomerate Rockefeller Standard Oil Company. They offered rebates on shipping rates that were ruinous to their competitors, if the oil company agreed to give these lines all their business.

emphasizes Norris's portrayal of him as an impersonal and uncaring petty autocrat.

The Plot. *The Octopus* is about a corporate body, the Pacific and Southwestern Railroad, which is virtually unregulated and holds all of the power in its conflict with the ranchers it serves. The railway trust owns a great deal of farmland on its right-of-way, which it leases to the wheat ranchers. The railroad charges outrageous tariffs for transporting the ranchers' wheat to market. Although railroad commissioners supposedly set shipping rates that can be appealed in the courts, the railroads control both the commissioners and the courts, leaving the ranchers unable to protest effectively.

Magnus Derrick, owner of the Los Muertos Ranch and the most prominent rancher in the area, ultimately succumbs to the utter hopelessness of the ranchers' situation. Although he is basically an upright and honest man, he pays bribes to have sympathetic railroad commissioners appointed. When his illegal act is revealed, Magnus loses what he cherishes most: his reputation.

Magnus's son Lyman, a San Francisco attorney, aspires to be governor. He, too, compromises his ideals by selling out to the railroad, hoping to gain their help in procuring the governorship. Magnus's other son, Harran, remains honest but is killed in a gunfight when the railroad attempts to take over part of Los Muertos, a major part of his heritage.

Harran is not the only one to die in the gunfight. Other farmers, whose land is controlled by the railroad, enter into the combat. Among those killed is Annixter, who switched from raising wheat to raising hops, only to have the railway substantially increase the tariff on hops just as Annixter needed to transport them to market. Magnus Derrick's tenant, Hooven, a German immigrant, and Osterman, who first proposes the bribery scheme that brings Derrick down, are also killed. In the end, Norris offers some moral justification: S. Behrman falls into the hold of a ship into which wheat is being poured for export, literally drowning in this sea of wheat.

Analysis. Despite his sympathy for the ranchers, Norris is not oblivious to the need for a railroad. He understands the necessary interdependence between those who must ship their products to market and those who provide, through a highly complex transportation system, the means for shipping them. Even as the protesting ranchers fall in a hail of bullets, Norris holds out hope that the future will be better.

Many naturalistic writers suggest that all is lost as the forces of a huge industrial complex unrelentingly crush the individuals in its path. Norris, however, states clearly that Truth will resurface "untouched, unassailable, and undefiled" as surely as next year's wheat.

SOURCES FOR FURTHER STUDY

Cargill, Oscar. Afterword to *The Octopus*, by Frank Norris. New York: Signet, 1964.

Folsom, James K. "The Wheat and the Locomotive: Norris and Naturalistic Esthetics." In *American Literary Naturalism: A Reassessment*, edited by Yoshinobu Hakutani and Lewis Fried. Heidelberg, Germany: Carl Winter-Universitatesverlag, 1975.

Hussman, Lawrence E. *Harbingers of a Century: The Novels of Frank Norris*. New York: Peter Lang, 1999.

McElrath, Joseph R., Jr. *Frank Norris Revisited*. New York: Twayne Publisher, 1992.

Pizer, Donald. *The Novels of Frank Norris*. Bloomington: Indiana University Press, 1966.

THE PIT: A STORY OF CHICAGO

Genre: Novel
Subgenre: Naturalism
Published: New York, 1903
Time period: 1890s
Setting: Chicago, Illinois

Themes and Issues. Frank Norris's second novel in his projected trilogy on growing and distributing wheat, *The Pit*, does not continue the narrative of the first, *The Octopus*. Rather, it deals with the buying and selling of wheat at the Chicago Board of Trade. On another, more intimate level, it tells how Laura Dearborn learns to love the man she marries. She remains faithful to him despite his considerable

The drama and fast money of the Chicago grain markets is captured in *A Flurry in Wheat*, an illustration that appeared in *Harper's Weekly* in October of 1880. In Norris's *The Pit*, Laura Dearborn finds her youthful idealism crushed in the wake of frenzied dealings and risky speculation.

neglect of her. She shuns Sheldon Corthell when he reappears at a crucial moment.

Laura's husband, Curtis Jadwin, flourishes in the rough-and-tumble world of commodity trading, where fortunes are made overnight and lost equally quickly. The other man in her life, Sheldon Corthell, is an artist who is more sensitive than her husband. Laura's conflict between the practical and the artistic is one that Norris experienced directly in the contrasting natures of each of his parents.

The Plot. Laura Dearborn, of whom the artist Sheldon Corthell is enamored, attends the opera with Sheldon one night as the guests of the Cresslers. Among the other guests is Curtis Jadwin, a successful trader in wheat on the Chicago Board of Trade. Jadwin, who rose from poverty to his current station, is immediately interested in Laura. She is intrigued by him, but she is not in love with him.

Jadwin calls in a loan on a valuable piece of Chicago acreage and ends up owning that property, soon selling it at a substantial profit. He uses this profit to buy additional real estate, eventually snowballing his investment into a real-estate empire in Chicago's wealthiest areas. He trades wheat on the Board of Trade, where his broker gives him a tip that the French will soon impose taxes on all imports, a move that will cause chaos in the wheat market.

Jadwin sells his position in wheat just in time and reaps huge profits, thus encouraging his speculations, even though the Cresslers warn him of the dangers of speculative activity, which once brought them to the brink of ruin.

Jadwin soon proposes marriage to Laura, who responds that she does not love anyone, a message she had also conveyed to Sheldon, who abandoned his romantic pursuit and sailed for Europe. Jadwin, a much more aggressive suitor, does not accept Laura's rejection and calls on her to discuss it. She changes her mind, and the two finally marry. The couple lives in high style as Jadwin's wealth increases, and Laura eventually begins to value Jadwin and what he has to offer her. To provide magnificently for her, however, Jadwin spends nearly all his time trading commodities, leaving Laura alone and often forlorn.

Laura dines with Sheldon when he returns from Europe. That very night, Jadwin comes home, having successfully completed a trade that has brought him a half-million dollars. He promises to give up his frenzied existence to spend more time with Laura. Eventually, however, he is lured back into trading, now as a bull rather than a bear, buying up shares in anticipation of rising prices. He struggles to corner the wheat market, buying as many shares as he can, but his efforts are thwarted by a wheat crop so plentiful that Jadwin's resources are soon exhausted. He is ruined financially.

Jadwin develops headaches caused by the pressure of his life. Mrs. Cressler tells Laura that her own husband also is unwell and invites Laura to visit her. When Laura gets to the Cresslers, Mrs. Cressler is not there. Laura wanders into the library, where she finds Mr. Cressler dead from a self-inflicted bullet wound. His suicide is triggered by financial losses induced in part by the unsettled market that Jadwin's unbridled speculation has created.

Jadwin, feeling responsible for Cressler's suicide, is now a broken man, bereft of his wealth and racked with guilt over the effects of his speculation. Laura tends to him during a prolonged illness, and the two move west for a new beginning in life. Despite their losses, they are happier than they have ever been.

Analysis. No matter how unhappy Norris's stories are, they usually have upbeat endings. This novel, Norris's most commercially successful work at the time of its publication, contains elements of melodrama. Deterministic forces lead to outcomes outside the control of the characters. Finally, though, the two leading characters head into the figurative sunset, where, Norris suggests, a better life awaits them.

Norris implies that wealth and the struggle to attain it jeopardize the happiness and satisfaction of people whose chief objective is gain. Jadwin enjoys having risen from poverty to wealth. Once he succeeds, however, his life deteriorates. Only when he loses most of his material possessions does he experience contentment.

SOURCES FOR FURTHER STUDY

Boyd, Jennifer. *Frank Norris: Spatial Form and Narrative Time*. New York: Peter Lang, 1993.

Buss, David M. *The Evolution of Desire*. New York: HarperCollins, 1994.

Dillingham, William B. *Frank Norris: Instinct and Art*. Lincoln: University of Nebraska Press, 1969.

Graham, Don, ed. *Critical Essays on Frank Norris*. Boston: G. K. Hall, 1980.

Mitchell, Mark, and Joseph R. McElrath, Jr. "Frank Norris's *The Pit*: Musical Elements as Biographical Evidence." *Papers in Language and Literature* 23 (Spring 1987): 161–174.

Peary, Gerald, and Roger Shatzkin. *The Classic American Novel and the Movies*. New York: Frederick Ungar, 1977.

Other Works

VANDOVER AND THE BRUTE (1914). The first words of *Vandover and the Brute* are "It was always a wonder to Vandover that he was able to recall so little of his past life." It has been suggested that these words encapsulate Norris's conception of the modern person.

Vandover is haunted by one memory of his past: that of his ailing mother dying in her husband's arms in a railway station in New York State as the family made its way from Boston to San Francisco. After that incident, the young Vandover has blocked the next five years out of his mind.

The loss of Vandover's mother is the motivating force for his deterioration. At the time Norris wrote this work in 1894, he himself was seeking a strong female influence. He had not yet met Jeannette Black, and he needed a female force in his life. This need carries over into his protagonist in this novel written during Norris's year at Harvard.

In essence, *Vandover and the Brute*—presumably written around the same time *McTeague* was—is a tract against self-indulgence. It reflects much of the Puritan outlook found in Norris's long ballad and first published work, *Yvernelle: A Tale of Feudal France*. The son of a rich San Francisco slumlord, Vandover, like Norris, wants to be an artist, but he lacks the self-discipline to succeed in that pursuit.

His precipitous downfall occurs after he seduces a trivial young woman who commits suicide out of guilt over their sexual encounter. When Vandover's father learns what his son has done, he dies, leaving Vandover his property. Vandover, however, eventually squanders and gambles away most of his inheritance and ends up as a custodian in a slum dwelling that his father once owned. He disintegrates rapidly, suffering from a condition known as lycanthropy, the delusion that one has become a wolf, and crawls about on all fours, howling.

MORAN OF THE LADY LETTY (1898).

Moran of the Lady Letty is the story of Ross Wilbur, son of a prominent San Francisco family and a Yale graduate, who is drugged and kidnapped aboard a ship. When he regains his senses, he is a short distance from a friend's yacht, but he becomes so intrigued by the boat on which he finds himself that he willingly remains on it.

Eventually, and improbably, Ross meets Moran, who has been shipwrecked. Norris says that Moran is "not made for men." She represents someone who believes in and lives Charles Darwin's concept of the survival of the fittest.

Ross is too much the gentleman to take sexual advantage of Moran, but in a graphic scene, he beats her viciously, suggesting that his violence is the sublimation of his unfulfilled sexual desire for her. This beating reflects a basic Puritanical streak that pervades much of Norris's writing, particularly in matters pertaining to sexuality. To Ross, Moran represents sexual temptation; the beating is both punishment and sublimation.

After the beating, Ross contends that he has conquered Moran, who loves him for it. Norris's concept of masculine superiority emerges fully, as it does in several of his other works. That having been settled, Ross and Moran plan to abandon the lives they had known and to go to Cuba together. Before they can do this, however, Moran is murdered by a Chinese laborer attempting to rob them.

Although this novel has few redeeming qualities, it is significant for its revelations about Norris's philosophy of relations between men and women. His views on gender were clearly set and are revealed in various ways throughout his writing. In both his life and his writing, Norris acknowledged his need for the influence of females, but he consistently viewed them as servile. Even his portrayal of Trina in *McTeague* suggests that a woman cannot truly be independent. Trina has her lottery winnings and her job, but in the end, McTeague, by killing her, becomes her superior physically. Ross, by beating Moran, gains control of her and emerges as her superior.

A MAN'S WOMAN (1900).

Lloyd Searight is a registered nurse attending the Arctic explorer Ward Bennett's best friend, who suffers from an infectious disease. Lloyd and Ward fall in love. Ward is stupid, reminiscent of McTeague, whose story was published a year earlier. Ward, closed-minded and dogmatic, has a weak memory. He also exercises control over people, although he has little to commend him as an authority figure.

Lloyd, in contrast, wants to do things rather than think, talk, or read about them. She is, however, far from resolute in this desire. Ward, in the masculine-superior role, convinces Lloyd to give up nursing his friend. Lloyd, the submissive woman, does Ward's bidding, wrongheaded though it may be.

Once Norris establishes Ward's superiority, albeit unconvincingly, Ward and Lloyd decide to marry and give up the work that has been central to their lives. Lloyd throws away a telegram asking her to take a challenging nursing case. Ward discards his book on Arctic exploration.

Lloyd, in Norris's view, abandons her life's work in yielding to Ward's masculine superiority. Ward's abandoning his career, on the other hand, is, in Norris's words, "hardly better than weakness." Norris calls Ward's capitulation an act of renunciation, but he calls Lloyd's capitulation surrender. Lloyd, in yielding to Ward, subjugates herself to him, but in doing so, she emerges as his moral superior.

Norris cannot allow the novel to end with Lloyd in the superior role. Although Ward has the opportunity to plant his flag as the first at the North Pole, he is reluctant to leave the comforts of home. Finally, however, a group of San Francisco businessmen approach him to encourage him to make the trip. When the proposed expedition is twenty thousand dollars short, Lloyd makes up the deficit. By doing so, she spurs Ward into accepting the challenge. He sets out for the Pole.

Most critics consider *A Man's Woman* among Norris's weaker novels. It is of little consequence artistically. It does, however, reveal a great deal about Norris's views of gender and, like *McTeague*, demonstrates his ability to present unsympathetic protagonists well.

Resources

The most comprehensive collection of Frank Norris's writing is found in the Frank Norris Collection of the Bancroft Library at the University of California, Berkeley. The Huntington Library in San Marino, California, also has a number of items of interest to Norris researchers, as well as resources of other naturalistic authors whose work is related to Norris's writing, including materials of such authors as Jack London, Theodore Dreiser, and Upton Sinclair.

Other valuable materials are found in the Butler Library of Columbia University, the Alderman Library of the University of Virginia, the California State Library at Sacramento, the Fisher Library of the University of Toronto, and the Library of Congress in Washington, D.C. The collections in the New York City and San Francisco Public Libraries have various Norris letters and manuscripts, as does the Beinecke Rare Book and Manuscript Library of Yale University. These libraries also have substantial collections related to the beginnings of literary naturalism in the United States. Other sources of interest to students of Frank Norris include the following:

The Frank Norris Society. An organization whose headquarters is located at Florida State University in Tallahassee, Florida. It has published *Frank Norris Studies* regularly since 1981. The Strozier Library at Florida State University has some Norris holdings.

Frank Norris (1870–1902). The William Dean Howells Society, dedicated to the study of Norris's friend and contemporary, features a Web site with a page devoted to Frank Norris with links to e-texts of Norris's works and other on-line resources. (http://www.gonzaga.edu/faculty/campbell/howells/norris.htm)

Project Gutenberg. This Internet resource provides the user with free, downloadable e-texts of many classic works, including several by Norris: *Blix*, *McTeague*, *Moran of the Lady Letty*, and *The Octopus*. (http://www.gutenberg.net)

R. BAIRD SHUMAN

Joyce Carol Oates

BORN: June 16, 1938, Lockport, New York
IDENTIFICATION: Prolific late-twentieth-century writer most known for her novels centering on the troubled and violent underside of American life.

Joyce Carol Oates is one of the most prolific writers in the whole of American literature. She has written a novel almost yearly since 1964 and has published numerous short stories, volumes of poetry, collections of plays, and literary studies and essays. In 1970 she won the National Book Award for her novel *them* (1969). In 1967 she received the first of several O. Henry Awards for excellence in short stories. Her 1994 novel *What I Lived For* was a finalist for both the PEN/Faulkner Award and the Pulitzer Prize. In 1996 she won the PEN/Malamud Award for achievement in the short story. She also served as Roger S. Berlind Distinguished Professor of Humanities at Princeton University.

The Writer's Life

Joyce Carol Oates was born on June 16, 1938, in Lockport, New York. She was reared in a rural, working-class Roman Catholic family. Her background hardly revealed the promise of an author who would, after three decades of consistent publication, produce more than seventy volumes. Frederick James Oates, her father, was a tool-and-die designer who dropped out of school in the seventh grade to go to work. Her mother, the former Caroline Bush, was a housewife.

Childhood and Education. Oates's working-class Roman Catholic upbringing in rural upstate New York—and the intensity and anguish of its religious and moral order—informs much of her work. Her formal education began inauspiciously enough in a one-room elementary school. Oates attended junior high in Lockport and high school outside Buffalo, New York. She was an outstanding high school student and earned a New York State Regents' Scholarship, which enabled her to enroll in Syracuse University in 1956. There she majored in English and minored in philosophy. A brilliant student, she graduated Phi Beta Kappa and was class valedictorian in 1960. Immediately upon receiving her bachelor's degree, Oates enrolled in the University of Wisconsin's graduate program and completed her master's degree in English in 1961.

The Writer Emerges. Even before Oates graduated from Syracuse, her writing talent was nationally recognized when she was named as one of the winners of *Mademoiselle* magazine's 1959 college fiction contest. From 1960 to 1964, she swiftly rose to literary prominence by publishing two collections of short stories and a novel, *With Shuddering Fall* (1964). In 1967 she won the first of her several O. Henry Awards for short fiction for her story "In the Region of Ice." Still in her twenties, she was emerging as an important writer who promised to make a major impact on twentieth-century American fiction.

Marriage and Teaching. While studying at the University of Wisconsin, Oates met and married Raymond J. Smith. In 1961 the couple spent a brief time in Texas and then moved to Detroit, Michigan,

These homes in Rockland County, New York, reflect the working-class and rural setting of Oates's childhood in Lockport, New York. The scenery of upstate New York and the rural people she knew as a child appear again and again in her work.

The prolific author sits in front of her white grand piano in her home in 1984, the same year her romantic ghost story *Mysteries of Winterthurn* was published.

where Smith joined the faculty of Wayne State University and Oates took a teaching position at the University of Detroit. The six years during which Oates taught in Detroit were to have a profound impact on her vision of American life. In 1967, the same year in which she was honored with a Guggenheim Fellowship, she took a faculty position at the University of Windsor in Ontario, Canada, where her husband had already been teaching for a year. She and her husband remained in Canada for eleven years. In addition to teaching and writing during this time, the couple founded the *Ontario Review: A North American Journal of the Arts*.

Major American Literary Figure. Although Oates taught in Canada for almost a decade, her writing from this period is clearly focused on the United States, its people, and their lives, especially in the Detroit area. The rough energy and violence of that city and the social and racial tribulations of the working class were the chief inspirations for the eight novels and eight short story collections that she published during her eleven years in Canada.

In addition to these works of fiction, Oates also published several collections of poems and critical works, as well as numerous articles in literary journals. Her output was prodigious, and on the basis of sheer volume alone she would have been considered a writer of considerable consequence. Critical recognition of her importance to American fiction came in 1970 with the National Book Award for *them*. With that award, Oates's reputation as a master of psychological realism and as a spellbinding storyteller of undiluted honesty was firmly established.

Writing Success and Academic Honors. In recognition of her literary and critical

FILMS BASED ON OATES'S STORIES

1985   *Smooth Talk*

1991   *Norman and the Killer*

1991   *Lies of the Twins* (TV)

1996   *Foxfire*

1999   *Getting to Know You*

Oates at a promotion for her 2000 novel *Blonde*, a fictional account of actress Marilyn Monroe's life. Writer Pamela Rosenthal wrote, "*Blonde*, of course, is anything but a feel-good book. It's eccentric, exhausting—and remarkable. Part horror, part melodrama, part wildly adventurous meditation, it sees in the dark—the way we all do at the movies—holding the remembered and cherished image in our eyes while we wait for the shutter to open and the frame to advance."

achievement, Oates was named the Roger S. Berlind Distinguished Professor of Humanities at Princeton University in 1978. She and her husband returned to live in the United States. In 1980 Oates established her mastery of a new form, the drama, with a collection entitled *Three Plays (1980)*. During the 1980s Oates displayed a postmodern twist by writing a series of "historic and gothic novels" cast as mysteries or romances or both. These novels of her "middle years as a writer" begin with the romance *Bellefleur* (1980) and include *A Bloodsmoor Romance* (1982) and the mystery/romance/ghost story *Mysteries of Winterthurn* (1984).

As the last decade of the twentieth century approached, Oates returned once again to the characters who, like herself, came of age in upstate New York in the 1950s. She also began to base some work on real-life events, such as her novels *Black Water* (1992), a fictional retelling of a scandal surrounding a prominent political figure; and *Foxfire: Confessions of a Girl Gang* (1993), a study of the social problem of girls' gangs.

Although Oates continued writing novels at a strong and consistent pace, she also investigated other forms, particularly drama. As companions to her *Three Plays*, she published three more drama collections: *Twelve Plays* (1991), *The Perfectionist and Other Plays* (1995), and *New Plays* (1998). *Black Water* was made into an opera, with music by John Duffy, and presented in Philadelphia in 1997 under the auspices of the American Music Theatre Festival. Along with her husband Raymond, the couple transformed the *Ontario Review* into a full-fledged publishing house, the Ontario Review Press.

Oates also continued her teaching duties at Princeton. The full significance of her place in American letters remains to be determined. Two novels of the 1990s, *Black Water* and *What I Lived For*, were nominated for the National Book Critics Circle Award and for the Pulitzer Prize. In 1996 Oates won the PEN/Malamud Award for Achievement in the short story.

HIGHLIGHTS IN OATES'S LIFE

1938 Joyce Carol Oates is born on June 16 in Lockport, New York.

1956 Graduates from high school and is awarded a New York State Regents' Scholarship; enters Syracuse University as an English major with a minor in philosophy.

1959 Wins *Mademoiselle*'s award for college fiction.

1960 Graduates as Phi Beta Kappa class valedictorian; enters graduate school at University of Wisconsin.

1961 Marries Raymond J. Smith; completes master's degree in English at University of Wisconsin.

1962 Joins faculty of the University of Detroit.

1964 Publishes first novel, *With Shuddering Fall*.

1967 Takes teaching position at University of Windsor in Ontario, Canada; receives her first O. Henry Award for short fiction; is awarded a Guggenheim Fellowship.

1968 Publishes first collection of poems, *Women in Love*.

1970 Receives National Book Award for novel *them*; her first play, *Sunday Dinner*, is produced in New York City.

1978 Oates accepts chair as Roger S. Berlind Distinguished Professor of Humanities at Princeton University.

1990 Receives Rae Award for the short story; shares Heideman Award for one-act plays.

1994 Her play *The Perfectionist* is nominated for the American Theater Critics Award.

1995 *What I Lived For* is finalist for Pulitzer Prize.

1996 Oates receives the PEN/Malamud Award for achievement in the short story.

1997 Opera version of *Black Water*, with music by John Duffy, is performed in Philadelphia.

The Writer's Work

There is hardly a literary form to which Joyce Carol Oates has not significantly contributed. She is a writer's writer, in that she sees all literary forms as meriting high-level attention. Nevertheless, she is perhaps best known as a novelist. After 1964 she published an average of at least one novel per year. This achievement is in addition to the volumes of short stories, poems, plays, essays, and literary studies she also published. Although Oates has experimented with a number of different novelistic genres—mysteries, romances, gothic tales, histories—her work is always characterized by strong psychological realism and a lyrical and highly personal use of language. Often her narrative technique is traditional, even when her vision of the world she presents is not.

Oates's American Vision. Oates is not a cheerful writer. Even her comedy is dark and foreboding. She avoids flatness and pessimism by seeing the world as filled with energy and extraordinary redemptive powers. At the same time, she sees much of the world's energy as seething with violence and evil. Indeed, a great portion of her work is centered on an unsentimental unearthing and examination of malevolence. To Oates, evil is found not only in people of high positions or from faraway places but also in ordinary working-class American men and women. Her characters are caught in economic and social traps with insufficient emotional and intellectual resources to elude the trap until they have been subjected to monstrous evil or have worked great wickedness on one another.

In presenting her dark mysteries of the human soul, Oates relentlessly pursues open, honest, and sometimes painful examinations of her characters' thoughts, words, and deeds.

This photograph of the slums of Detroit, Michigan, represents the trap in which so many of Oates's characters are caught. The scene, void of intellectual stimulation and resources, reveals a dirt path to a future that is less than promising.

She is concerned with the dark underside of society and the proclivity of both men and women to engage in, or at least tolerate, unmitigated evil. She is also interested in the resilience of the human soul in transcending such evil, especially when aided by the extraordinary power of love.

People, Places, and Themes.

As a writer with such a prodigious output, it is not surprising that Oates, while clearly focusing on the American experience, does not limit herself to characters of one social class or type or gender. Her works include the sweep of American culture throughout the nineteenth and twentieth centuries, from nineteenth-century middle- to upper-class persons in *Mysteries of Winterthurn* to twentieth-century urban blacks and whites in *them*.

Club Night, a 1907 oil painting by artist George Wesley Bellows, explores the interest of the onlookers after a boxer receives a crippling blow from his opponent. The work reflects the subject of Oates's 1987 novel *You Must Remember This*. Like Oates, Bellows was known for his sinister portrayals, and also like Oates, he was passionate about representing contemporary urban life. He is, as the title reveals, the focus of her 1995 work of nonfiction, *George Bellows: American Artist*.

As a woman, Oates might be expected to write about the female experience, and she has done so movingly. However, she has also masterfully portrayed the male psyche in such characters as the small-time urban politicians in *What I Lived For*, the high-living con men in *My Heart Laid Bare* (1998), the college professors in *American Appetites* (1989), and the professional boxers in *You Must Remember This* (1987).

Oates's characters are usually working-class or rural men and women living in upstate New York or northeastern industrial cities such as Detroit. They are trapped by their inherited socioeconomic situations and thus lack the cultural resources to escape their predicaments, even when they might have some personal strengths, financial wherewithal, or encouragement from teachers or friends. A typical Oates character is a working-class woman, such as those found in her novels *The Rise of Life on Earth* (1991) and *Because It Is Bitter, and Because It Is My Heart* (1990). The woman may also belong to a rural society, as in *We Were the Mulvaneys* (1996).

In Oates's later novels, such as *Man Crazy* (1997) and *First Love* (1996), young women endure sexual molestation, physical torture, and enslavement. Oates fearlessly explores the relationship between abuser and abused and the numbing fear that seals the mouths of victims. Still, the tenacity of the human spirit is seen in the triumph over these evils by Ingrid Boone, the young heroine of *Man Crazy*. A similar salvation is attained by Marya Knauer, famous author and member of the intellectual elite, in *Marya: A Life* (1986). Sometimes Oates's women are not victims but perpetrators, as in two powerful studies of women engaged in evil: the novel *Foxfire: Confessions of A Girl Gang* and the play *Bad Girls* (1998).

Although characters are important in Oates's work, locale is equally significant. Always attentive to the details of the setting and skillful in conveying its presence and quality, she uses

SOME INSPIRATIONS BEHIND OATES'S WORK

Joyce Carol Oates's childhood landscape of upstate New York and its people and places are a major influence in Oates's fiction. The scenery of upstate New York is a constant in her work, as are the rural people she knew as a child. The Roman Catholic traditions of her family are also apparent in her art.

The excellent education she received at Syracuse and the University of Wisconsin also informs her work. The literature and philosophy she studied in her formal education springs up in the style and content of her writing.

Above all in Oates's writing, there is the city of Detroit, with its energy and violence, which Oates came to know while teaching at the University of Detroit. She said that Detroit is her "quintessential American city," and it is the locale of many of her stories. In 1971 Oates reported having a mystical experience, and the growing presence of the supernatural or the mysterious can be seen in her work after that date.

A member of Detroit's Gang Squad frisks a man on a busy street while pedestrians watch in 1982. The violence, energy, and raw thirst for survival found on the streets of Detroit have made for compelling material in Oates's works, which is why she has labeled Detroit her "quintessential American city."

the energies provided by time and place to drive the story forward. Her locales vary from farmhouse to urban ghetto, from historic mansions to reclaimed churches, as in *Mysteries of Winterthurn* or *My Heart Laid Bare*. Her favorite locales are urban industrial centers, where the underprivileged's struggle to survive frequently boils over into brutality and violence. However, Oates is aware that other places and climates also harbor similar evils and that even Americans of the highest social positions—from academics to holders of national office—are not exempt from wickedness. She explores such people and places in novels such as *American Appetites* and *Black Water*.

BIBLIOGRAPHY

Bender, Eileen Teper. *Joyce Carol Oates: Artist in Residence*. Bloomington: Indiana University Press, 1987.

Bloom, Harold, ed. *Modern Critical Views: Joyce Carol Oates*. New York: Chelsea House, 1987.

Creighton, Joanne. *Joyce Carol Oates: Novels of the Middle Years*. New York: Twayne Publishers, 1992.

Daly, Brenda Lavish. *Self-Deceptions: The Novels of Joyce Carol Oates*. Jackson: University of Mississippi Press, 1996.

Friedman, Ellen G. *Joyce Carol Oates*. New York: Frederick Ungar, 1980.

Johnson, Greg. *Invisible Writer: A Biography of Joyce Carol Oates*. New York: Dutton, 1998.

———. *Understanding Joyce Carol Oates*. New York: Dutton, 1987.

Lercangee, Francine. *Joyce Carol Oates: An Annotated Bibliography*. New York: Garland, 1986.

Malazzo, Lee. *Conversations with Joyce Carol Oates*. Jackson: University of Mississippi Press, 1987.

Watanabe, Mary Ann. *Love Eclipsed: Joyce Carol Oates' Faustian Moral Vision*. New York: University Press of America, 1998.

LONG FICTION

- 1964 With Shuddering Fall
- 1967 A Garden of Earthly Delights
- 1968 Expensive People
- 1969 them
- 1971 Wonderland
- 1973 Do with Me What You Will
- 1975 The Assassins: A Book of Hours
- 1976 Childwold
- 1976 The Triumph of the Spider Monkey
- 1978 Son of the Morning
- 1979 Unholy Loves
- 1979 Cybele
- 1980 Bellefleur
- 1981 Angel of Light
- 1982 A Bloodsmoor Romance
- 1984 Mysteries of Winterthurn
- 1985 Solstice
- 1986 Marya: A Life
- 1987 Lives of the Twins (as Rosamond Smith)
- 1987 You Must Remember This
- 1989 American Appetites
- 1989 Soul/Mate (as Smith)
- 1990 Because It Is Bitter, and Because It Is My Heart
- 1990 I Lock My Door upon Myself
- 1990 Nemesis (as Smith)
- 1991 The Rise of Life on Earth
- 1992 Black Water
- 1992 Snake Eyes (as Smith)
- 1993 Foxfire: Confessions of a Girl Gang
- 1994 What I Lived For
- 1995 You Can't Catch Me (as Smith)
- 1995 Zombie
- 1996 We Were the Mulvaneys
- 1996 First Love
- 1997 Man Crazy
- 1998 My Heart Laid Bare
- 1999 Broke Heart Blues
- 1999 Starr Bright Will Be with You (as Smith)
- 2000 Blonde

SHORT FICTION

- 1963 By the North Gate
- 1966 Upon the Sweeping Flood
- 1970 The Wheel of Love
- 1972 Marriages and Infidelities
- 1974 The Goddess and Other Women
- 1974 The Hungry Ghosts
- 1974 Where Are You Going, Where Have You Been?
- 1975 The Poisoned Kiss
- 1975 The Seduction
- 1976 Crossing the Border
- 1977 Night-Side
- 1978 All the Good People I've Left Behind
- 1979 The Lamb of Abyssalia
- 1980 A Sentimental Education
- 1984 Last Days
- 1986 Raven's Wing
- 1988 The Assignation
- 1991 Heat and Other Stories
- 1992 Where Is Here?
- 1994 Haunted: Tales of the Grotesque
- 1994 Will You Always Love Me?
- 1998 The Collector of Hearts

PLAYS

- 1970 Sunday Dinner
- 1974 Miracle Play
- 1980 Three Plays
- 1991 In Darkest America: Two Plays
- 1991 I Stand Before You Naked
- 1991 Twelve Plays
- 1995 The Perfectionist and Other Plays
- 1998 New Plays

POETRY

- 1968 Women in Love
- 1969 Anonymous Sins
- 1970 Love and Its Derangements
- 1973 Angel Fire
- 1975 The Fabulous Beasts
- 1978 Women Whose Lives Are Food, Men Whose Lives Are Money
- 1982 Invisible Woman: New and Selected Poems, 1970–1982
- 1984 The Luxury of Sin
- 1987 The Time Traveler
- 1996 Tenderness

NONFICTION

- 1972 The Edge of Impossibility: Tragic Forms in Literature
- 1973 The Hostile Sun: The Poetry of D. H. Lawrence
- 1974 New Heaven, New Earth: The Visionary Experience in Literature
- 1981 Contraries: Essays
- 1983 The Profane Art: Essays and Reviews
- 1987 On Boxing
- 1988 (Woman) Writer: Occasions and Opportunities
- 1995 George Bellows: American Artist

EDITED TEXTS

- 1972 Scenes from American Life: Contemporary Short Fiction
- 1979 The Best American Short Stories of 1979 (with Shannon Ravenel)
- 1982 Night Walks: A Bedside Companion
- 1983 First Person Singular: Writers on Their Craft
- 1991 The Best American Essays
- 1992 The Oxford Book of American Short Stories
- 1996 American Gothic Tales

CHILDREN'S LITERATURE

- 1998 Come Meet Muffin

Reader's Guide to Major Works

MYSTERIES OF WINTERTHURN

Genre: Novel
Subgenre: Romantic ghost story
Published: New York, 1984
Time period: Late nineteenth century
Setting: Fictitious upstate New York town

Themes and Issues. One of Joyce Carol Oates's gothic mysteries, *Mysteries of Winterthurn* explores the intricacies of the human personality and its tendency to embrace both good and evil. The novel asks whether human beings can ever be simple enough and completely pure, rather than a complex of intellect and passion, good and evil. Oates's choice of the detective genre, especially that of the nineteenth century, makes an excellent vehicle for her theme.

The central character, the detective whose nature is defined almost entirely by his intellect and his belief in a beneficent God, labors through three mystery cases, each entangled with a sense of unknowable evil. In the end he succeeds neither in bringing the evildoers to justice nor in simplifying his own soul, for he ultimately succumbs to an overpowering passion for a woman capable of the most atrocious and unspeakable deeds. He forsakes his intellectual profession, ignores the pure and abiding love of one woman, and begins the new twentieth century in a marriage to a woman hardly likely to look back to Victorian ideals.

The Plot. The novel is divided into three parts, each centering on a different mystery at three crucial points in the life of Xavier Kilgarvan, a detective reminiscent of such masters as Sherlock Holmes. Each of the novel's three mysteries involves a puzzling killing, sometimes a multiple killing, taking place under eerie circumstances. Each mystery serves to reveal further the deep, dark, and complex passion that exists between Xavier and his beautiful cousin, Perdita.

The first mystery concerns the death of an infant in Glen Marw Manor. The death might have been the work of the infant's mother, but it might have been caused by malignant spirits inhabiting the Manor. The schoolboy Xavier Kilgarvan is determined to be a detective and sets out to the Manor to investigate. There he

This example of Victorian trick photography (ca. 1860), a female ghost floating above a baby's crib, mimics the gothic eeriness of the first of three mysteries in Oates's chilling novel *Mysteries of Winterthurn*.

meets his twelve-year-old cousin, Perdita, with whom he falls in love. Xavier finally solves the mystery. However, the solution contains such terrible and loathsome family secrets that he cannot bring himself to make the solution public, and he leaves Winterthurn to practice his profession elsewhere.

Between the first and second mysteries there are other terrible events relating to Glen Marw Manor, but the crimes that draw Xavier back to Winterthurn involve the mutilated bodies of several young working-class women discovered in a desolate spot called the "Devil's Half-Acre." Xavier solves the mystery to his great personal dismay, as more dreadful family secrets are revealed. Moreover, he is once again rejected by Perdita.

At forty and at the height of his professional reputation, Xavier returns a third time to Winterthurn to work on the case of the "Bloodstained Bridal Gown." He unravels the twisted events, but he is forced to forsake his profession in order to reconcile what he now knows about his family's curse with his undying passion for Perdita. He chooses Perdita, who comes to him riding on a bicycle, the image of the new, liberated woman of the twentieth century.

Analysis. Oates is telling a ghost story, and as such she asks readers to acknowledge that there are experiences beyond the present, beyond the palpable, and beyond human logic. Her choice of a detective—a person of pure intellect dependent upon his ability to reason—as the story's hero becomes the more ironic as the narrative progresses. For each of his successes in solving mysteries, Xavier is left with more and more knowledge unable to be treated on a purely intellectual plane. Finally, he yields to the one transcendent emotion and gives his life over in love to his cousin, Perdita.

Oates is also creating a work of history written as it might be told one hundred years ago, and she is asking readers to relive that history to appreciate what is valuable in it and to better understand what should be forgotten about it. Perdita is a new woman, lost to Victorian ideals, but awake to a new century. To accept her means not only to enter a new void but to leave the old evils behind. Moreover, accepting Perdita means embracing the complexity of the human experience, the human capacity for both good and evil. This Xavier does.

Oates deals with the themes of human complexity and of the rejection of simple Victorian values, by critiquing Victorian attitudes toward sex and gender roles through the use of a nineteenth-century narrative style reflecting that century's attitudes toward women. Thus, the novel is postmodern, feminist, and subtle. Oates fashions a fascinating story, loaded with wry humor, as she lovingly emulates a borrowed style and, at the same time, manages to satirize that bygone style as well as its era.

SOURCES FOR FURTHER STUDY

Creighton, Joanne. *Joyce Carol Oates: Novels of the Middle Years.* New York: Twayne Publishers, 1992.

Malazzo, Lee. *Conversations with Joyce Carol Oates.* Jackson: University of Mississippi Press, 1987.

Waller, G. F. *Dreaming America: Obsession and Transcendence in the Fiction of Joyce Carol Oates.* Baton Rouge: Louisiana State University Press, 1997.

them

Genre: Novel
Subgenre: Social criticism
Published: New York, 1969
Time period: 1960s
Setting: Detroit, Michigan

Themes and Issues. Oates's National Book Award–winning novel *them* presents the overwhelming difficulties of poverty in an American industrial city. Densely detailed, the novel relates one family's struggle with the relentless poverty that continually breeds violence and spiritual devastation. Yet, as in all her works, Oates holds up the indomitable spirit of the human heart and the capacity for survival of even the most ill-treated. Her characters persevere and even triumph in some small measure over the vicissitudes of life in the slums. For Oates, human love is certainly the major factor in this triumph.

The Plot. Oates follows the lives of Loretta Wendell, her three children—Maureen, Jules, and Betty—and the various people in their lives. The novel begins with Loretta as a teenager preparing to meet a young man, whom she later brings back to her family's apartment and takes to bed. Her brother shoots the young man. Loretta flees the apartment, meets a policeman, and seduces and marries him. This couple have the three children at the center of the novel.

Betty is less important to the story than are her brother and sister. Ultimately, the policeman husband leaves Loretta, who remarries. Jules struggles to make whatever money he can; he works at night and tries his hand at burglary but is caught, robbed, and beaten by a policeman. Maureen begins to practice prostitution and is discovered and nearly beaten to death by her stepfather. In a catatonic state for thirteen months, Maureen is nursed by both her brother and her uncle. Jules holds several questionable jobs, and finally, after meeting Nandine, a teenage daughter of a wealthy family, he follows her suggestion and runs off with her to Texas. The two manage to survive because Jules commits various thieveries, some involving considerable violence. Jules becomes ill, and Nandine returns to Detroit.

In the meantime, Maureen has recovered and finished high school. She has found a job as a typist and attends college at night. She seduces her English teacher and insists he marry her, even though he is already married and the father of three children. Jules has returned to Detroit, where he is fortunate enough to find a job with another of his uncles. However, he meets Nandine once again and while they are making love, Nandine shoots him and herself.

Both survive, but Jules now has no job. He makes his way as a pimp, exploiting a young girl he has seduced, and he is befriended by certain revolutionary faculty members at Wayne State University. Suddenly, the Detroit riots break out, and Jules becomes a spokesman for the downtrodden. The novel ends with Jules and Maureen saying goodbye. She is soon to have a baby; he is off to the West Coast to work in some social capacity about which he knows nothing. Both clearly love one another; both are also anxious to be rid of their past.

Analysis. *them* is a work of social history that Oates claims is based upon a true story. The novel is perhaps her most powerful presentation of the destructive nature of American inner-city life. The novel's characters are poor, uneducated, and virtually without hope. They survive because they need to survive in order to aid those they love. They want to escape, to leave *them*, but they also realize that their loved ones have made it possible for them to live into adulthood. This is a novel about the power of humankind to triumph against overwhelming odds and to survive the most dehumanizing treatment.

Oates's 1969 novel, *them*, exposes the darkness of street life in Detroit while illuminating the support two siblings give each other and the power of the human spirit to overcome the horrific obstacles inner-city life creates.

SOURCES FOR FURTHER STUDY

Friedman, Ellen G. *Joyce Carol Oates*. New York: Frederick Ungar, 1980.

Grant, Mary Kathryn. *The Tragic Vision of Joyce Carol Oates*. Durham, N.C.: Duke University Press, 1978.

Wesley, Marilyn C. *Refusal and Transgression in Joyce Carol Oates*. Westport, Conn.: Greenwood Press, 1993.

WHAT I LIVED FOR

Genre: Novel
Subgenre: Character study
Published: New York, 1994
Time period: One Memorial Day weekend in the late twentieth century
Setting: Fictitious upstate New York city

Themes and Issues. *What I Lived For* covers four days in the life of Jerome "Corky" Corcoran. Corky is an American prototype: a rising political operator, a popular money-juggling man's man who is also a successful womanizer. Throughout the weekend, readers literally live and breathe, sweat and strain with Corky as he wheels and deals to keep his financial empire from disintegrating and his love life from unraveling.

Oates uses Corky as a barometer for the study of human strength and weakness, hunger and carnality, desire and corruption. Corky is an ambitiously small-time incarnation of the American national myth of manhood and success. Oates dissects this myth and at the same time captures the energy and relentless drive that characterize persons who pursue this myth, as well as the doom that ultimately awaits them.

The Plot. Because Oates's purpose is to study intensively an individual over a limited period, *What I Lived For* is not intricately plotted. Corcoran, a wheeler-dealer in low-rent real estate, is a city councilman for Union City, a dying urban center in upstate New York. He engages in questionable activities, as do his political associates Oscar Slattery, Union City's mayor, and Slattery's son, Vic, a U.S. Congressman.

A bottle of whiskey and two glasses reflect much of Corky Corcoran's world in Oates's 1994 novel *What I Lived For*. Corky, a boozer and a womanizer, lives his life by trying to avoid any aspect of it that could be meaningful.

The novel begins in Corky's childhood, with a prologue describing Corky's father's shooting death over a shady political business deal. Many years later, in the novel proper, readers enter Corky's mind on the Friday of a Memorial Day weekend and remain exclusively in Corky's consciousness until Monday evening. The action starts in a traffic jam, as Corky is on his way to a sexual tryst with his current mistress, and follows him to the local athletic club as he discusses his shaky financial dealings with his financial advisor.

Corky spends the remainder of the day in his real-estate office and in a visit to his stepdaughter's apartment, which he enters uninvited. Snooping through her things, he learns that his friend Vic Slattery, though married, is probably romantically involved with his stepdaughter's African-American girlfriend, Melissa. Corky then spends the evening drinking and misses a dinner invitation. On Saturday Corky learns of the suicide of his stepdaughter's friend Melissa.

The next three days are taken up with visits with his stepdaughter, a couple of shady business deals, some heavy drinking that causes him to miss more dinner invitations, sexual adventures with a young friend of his stepdaughter and with his former wife, and finally a political reception at which Vic Slattery is shot at by Corky's stepdaughter, using a gun that she has stolen from Corky. Corky inadvertently steps in the way of the bullets and saves Slattery's life. The novel ends with Corky recovering from his wounds and getting ready to reenter his competitive, rough-and-tumble life

Analysis. *What I Lived For* begins with an assassination and ends with an assassination attempt. Inside this frame of murder, readers are invited to spend four days with Corky in the virtual hell of Union City, of which Corky says, "Union City is in a fiscal crisis, Union City is in a crime crisis, Union City is in a moral crisis, Union City *is* a crisis." The same can be said of Corky. He is, for Oates, quintessentially American—a small-time politician and slum lord, always in a crisis, always on the edge of moral and financial disaster, closed-minded but filled with a driving energy and optimism.

Corky is "not comfortable inside his head," and neither are readers, but that is where Oates has put them. Corky drives himself to lose consciousness—drinking too much, engaging in promiscuous and usually loveless sex with several women over a brief span of time, turning business deals for the sake of dealing, doing anything to avoid thinking. As commentary on the American Dream and those who dream it, as commentary on the way in which the American male is driven, as commentary on America as a form of living hell, Oates's novel makes vivid the male myths as they are conceived and lived in American cities.

SOURCES FOR FURTHER STUDY

Johnson, Greg. *Invisible Writer: A Biography of Joyce Carol Oates*. New York: Dutton, 1998.

Waller, G. F. *Dreaming America: Obsession and Transcendence in the Fiction of Joyce Carol Oates*. Baton Rouge: Louisiana State University Press, 1997.

Watanabe, Mary Ann. *Love Eclipsed: Joyce Carol Oates' Faustian Moral Vision*. New York: University Press of America, 1998.

Other Works

BAD GIRLS (1998). A play adapted from a short story of the same title, *Bad Girls* was first produced by the Georgia Repertory Theatre in 1995 and later published in *New Plays* (1998). It belongs among the more realistic pieces of Joyce Carol Oates's writing, unlike such highly lyric dramas as *Black Water*. As in Oates's novel *Foxfire: Confessions of a Girl Gang*, a group of girls, here teenage sisters, deliberately ruin the life of a man who comes between them and their single mother.

Marietta has three daughters and works as a clerk in an automotive repair garage; her life is difficult. Of her daughters, Icy in particular is rebellious and out of hand. Still, life is manageable, and Marietta is fortunate finally to meet a good and gentle man, a retired Army major. She invites him to supper, and, as a bachelor, he is somewhat uncomfortable in a house full of women. Thus, the evening is filled with awkward good humor, and it appears that a warm, romantic comedy will follow.

However, Icy and her sisters cannot endure the thought of a man intruding into their world, and in a terrible turn of events they accuse the major of sexually molesting them, a false charge about which the man cannot prove his innocence. Marietta loses her chance for an adult life; the major loses his reputation. Nevertheless, there is a bittersweet twist to the play: Marietta continues to give her love to her children as any good mother would. Again, as in so much of her work, Oates holds up the complexities of the human heart, its startling capacity for evil, and its equally powerful capacity for love.

BLACK WATER (1992). One of Oates's shorter novels, *Black Water* deserves special consideration for three reasons. First, as a short novel it illustrates Oates's great contributions to the genre of short fiction, for which she has received many honors. Second, it is an excellent

Edvard Munch's *A Summer Night on the Beach* depicts a beach scene not unlike the last scene the character Kelly Kelleher would have witnessed in Oates's hauntingly realistic first-person account of the isolation and desolation of a drowning woman in *Black Water*.

example of her ability to create lavish lyrical prose. Third, *Black Water*, in its 1997 opera adaptation, converts the novel's lyric prose into gripping verse that reveals Oates's considerable gifts as a poet.

As a piece of short fiction, *Black Water* is a classic example of Oates's skill at narrative economy. Although her works can be expansive in scope, *Black Water* comes quickly to its terrible moment, the sudden death of a young and beautiful woman. The opera version also is a remarkable example of artistic economy. Moreover, comparing the novel and the opera (published in *New Plays*, 1998) is an excellent study in literary forms.

The novel is told almost exclusively through the first-person viewpoint of Kelly Kelleher, the young woman who becomes infatuated with a charismatic U.S. senator whom she meets at a garden party and whose invitation to a tryst she accepts unhesitatingly. As they are driving, the senator, who has been drinking too much, loses control of his car, and they are thrown off a bridge. The senator thinks only of himself and kicks free of the car, leaving Kelly to drown. Readers spend the last gruesome moments of Kelly's life with her as she dies in the black water. Some of Oates's most gorgeous prose is used to present the subjective viewpoint of the drowning woman in the novel.

The opera uses little of the first-person viewpoint, gaining its subjectivity from the music and certain dramatic and theatrical conventions. Oates introduces a chorus that sings Kelly's feelings. She also calls upon the lyric devices of the theater, such as a scrim, or transparent curtain, to create an atmosphere of romantic love. Finally, she turns from lyric prose to lean-bodied poetry in the libretto for the opera. Whether in poetry or prose, narrative or drama, Oates continues to pursue her relentless illumination of the darkest places of the human soul. In *Black Water*, which echoes a real American scandal, she presents the American ideal—a brilliant man, gifted with money, power, social position and intelligence—a leader of men who exploits the gullibility of a young woman by seducing her and then, when an accident occurs, abandons her to a terrible death.

Resources

The most useful source of information on Joyce Carol Oates is the Joyce Carol Oates Archive at Syracuse University's Department of Special Collections. The archive includes business and personal correspondence, journals, typescript and holograph manuscripts for essays, novels, plays, poems, periodicals, photographs, and reviews. Other sources of interest to students of Joyce Carol Oates include the following:

Documentary. As part of its half-hour documentary series on contemporary writers, *The Writer*, the New York State Writers Institute filmed a thirty-minute feature on Oates, with public readings, interviews, and seminars. Information can be found at the Web site. (http://www.albany.edu/writers-inst/)

Audio Recordings. The lyric opera version of Oates's novel, *Black Water: A New American Opera* (1998), starring Karen Burlingame and Patrick Mason, is available on compact disc from the Audio Theatre Series. Several of Oates's novels have been recorded and are available in audiocassette form, including *Because It Is Bitter, and Because It Is My Heart* (1990), *Blonde* (2000, abridged), *A Bloodsmoor Romance* (1982), and *Solstice* (1985).

Interviews. The on-line magazine *Salon* features interviews with Oates. Available are one concerning her 1995 novel *Zombie* (http://www.salon.com/06/departments/litchat.html) and another concerning her 2000 novel *Blonde* (http://www.salon.com/books/feature/2000/04/18/blonde/index.html?CP=SAL&DN=110).

AUGUST W. STAUB

Tim O'Brien

BORN: October 1, 1946, Austin, Minnesota
IDENTIFICATION: Late-twentieth-century novelist best known for his portrayals of U.S. participation in the war in Vietnam.

Tim O'Brien has been called the most powerful American writer to portray the U.S. involvement in Vietnam from the point of view of those who did the fighting. His own United States Army experience in Vietnam led first to the essays that became *If I Die in a Combat Zone, Box Me Up and Ship Me Home* (1973), and then to *Going After Cacciato* (1978) and *The Things They Carried* (1990). *Going After Cacciato* won the National Book Award in 1979. His later novels, specifically *In the Lake of the Woods* (1994) and *Tomcat in Love* (1998), also use themes connected with the war. Although they have their admirers, they did not meet with the almost unanimous critical approval that greeted his earlier work.

The Writer's Life

William Timothy O'Brien was born on October 1, 1946, in Austin, Minnesota. His father, also named William Timothy O'Brien, was an insurance salesman. His mother, Ava Schultz O'Brien, taught school. Both his parents had military backgrounds, having served in the United States Navy during World War II. When O'Brien was nine, his family moved to Worthington, Minnesota, where he spent the rest of his youth.

Childhood. O'Brien described Worthington, a small farming town in rural southern Minnesota, as the essence of dullness. Known as the "Turkey Capital of the World," the town celebrates "Turkey Day," when local farmers herd turkeys down Worthington's main street, and O'Brien paints a comic picture of this festival in both his fiction and his memoirs. Nevertheless, it was in Worthington, during an ordinary childhood, that O'Brien first felt the desire to write.

At ten years of age O'Brien came across a book in the local library that he said was as important to his becoming a writer as any of the classics. In this book, *Larry of the Little League*, O'Brien—himself a mediocre Little League shortstop—immediately recognized the possibility of remaking his own lackluster baseball career as a work of fiction. The story that he wrote after reading *Larry of the Little League* charted the fabulous Little League deeds of

A quintessential image of small-town Americana, men chase turkeys during a Thanksgiving Day parade in Minnesota in 1955. The Vietnam War was to come as a crushing blow to the innocence and idealism that marked the era.

O'Brien poses at his computer with his trademark baseball cap. He learned at an early age that his joint passions—Little League and writing—could intersect, one embellishing the other and each easing the shortcomings of reality.

"Timmy," a boy who was very much like himself, except for his remarkable talent at playing shortstop. It was O'Brien's first experience with what has become an important theme in his work—the idea that fiction allows writers to reshape reality as they need or wish it to be.

O'Brien attended Macalester College in St. Paul, Minnesota, during the early years of the U.S. military involvement in Vietnam. Young men were being drafted into the Army, but O'Brien for the most part ignored the war, believing on one hand that his excellent academic standing and his plans for graduate school would keep him from being drafted, and hoping on the other hand that if he ignored it, the war would disappear. He opposed the war on principle, however, and he participated in a few low-key, on-campus antiwar protests and also campaigned for the popular antiwar presidential candidate Senator Eugene McCarthy.

At Macalester O'Brien majored in political science and was active in campus politics, working for the liberalization of campus social restrictions and for academic reform. In his senior year he was president of the student body. He graduated with high honors in 1968 and planned to enter Harvard University as a graduate student in government in the following fall. Instead he received a draft notice.

Military Life. O'Brien spent the summer after graduation considering what to do about the draft. His family was supportive but noncommittal; the decision was his to make. O'Brien gave serious thought to dodging the draft by going to Canada, but he finally concluded that to leave the country would embarrass his family and label him a coward. O'Brien called his decision on this issue another sort of cowardice. In any event, by the winter of 1969 he was a private first class with Alpha Company, in the Fifth Battalion of the Forty-sixth Infantry stationed in Quang Ngai province, arriving there less than a year after the My Lai massacre of approximately 350 South Vietnamese women and children which had been carried out by Charlie Company, under the command of First Lieutenant William L. Calley.

O'Brien had nothing to do with the massacre, which had come under public investigation during the fall of 1969, but his company's area of patrol included the My Lai area. He became aware of the incident and used it as part of the background for his novel *In the Lake of the Woods*. In fact, O'Brien said that he was not aware that he killed anyone during his time in Vietnam, but that seeing the wounding and deaths of comrades and friends led him to feel the sort of anger that he believed could easily lead a person to retaliate against the enemy in any way possible.

O'Brien was discharged from the Army in 1970 after attaining the rank of sergeant. He was awarded a Purple Heart for a superficial shrapnel wound he received in the line of duty. Back in the United States, he enrolled at Harvard as a graduate student in government and prepared to pick up his interrupted academic career.

Writing. During his Harvard years, O'Brien held two summer internships with the *Washington Post*. In the 1973–1974 academic year he took a leave of absence to report for the *Washington Post* on national affairs. After publishing some essays about his war experiences in *Esquire* magazine, he concluded that he wanted to spend his time writing. Although he came to dislike political reporting, he said that his experience with the *Washington Post* gave him a good introduction to the discipline of writing and meeting deadlines. In 1973 O'Brien published his first book, a collection of war essays, *If I Die in a Combat Zone, Box Me Up and Ship Me Home*. Critics praised the book's unadorned prose style, although in later years O'Brien expressed distaste for the collection, issuing a revised edition in 1989.

Shortly before O'Brien discontinued his studies at Harvard in 1976, he published his first novel, *Northern Lights* (1975). Although it is not explicitly a war novel, the book examines some themes that have been important in O'Brien's considerations of warfare, especially the idea of courage. It was his second novel, *Going After Cacciato*, that gave true fictional expression to O'Brien's ideas about the war and also won the National Book Award in 1979. *The Nuclear Age* (1985), a novel about an ex-peace activist, received less enthusiastic reviews. O'Brien called *The Things They Carried*, a collection of stories and essays published in 1990, his best work.

In 1994, just before the publication of *In the Lake of the Woods*,

Bearing the profile of George Washington, the Purple Heart is awarded to those wounded in battle. To have escaped the war with only a minor injury was no insignificant feat for O'Brien.

HIGHLIGHTS IN O'BRIEN'S LIFE

1946 William Timothy O'Brien is born on October 1 in Austin, Minnesota.

1968 Graduates summa cum laude with a bachelor's degree in political science from Macalester College in St. Paul, Minnesota; is drafted for service in Vietnam.

1969 Arrives in Quang Ngai province, Vietnam.

1970 Is discharged from Army; receives Purple Heart for shrapnel wound; returns to United States and undertakes graduate studies in government at Harvard University.

1973 Marries Ann Elizabeth Weller; takes leave of absence from Harvard to do political reporting for *Washington Post*; publishes war memoir, *If I Die in a Combat Zone, Box Me Up and Ship Me Home*.

1974 Returns to Harvard to complete dissertation; begins to write and publish about his war experiences.

1975 Publishes first novel, *Northern Lights*.

1976 Drops out of Harvard.

1978 Publishes *Going After Cacciato*.

1979 Receives National Book Award for *Going After Cacciato*.

1985 Publishes *The Nuclear Age*.

1990 Publishes short fiction and memoir, *The Things They Carried*; is divorced from wife.

1994 Makes return visit to Vietnam; publishes *In the Lake of the Woods*; stops writing for a period of introspection.

1998 Publishes *Tomcat in Love*.

O'Brien made a return trip to Vietnam, visiting the areas where his company had operated, including My Lai. The wrenching experience left O'Brien in a deep depression, which he recorded in a very personal essay, "The Vietnam in Me," for *The New York Times* on October 2, 1994. Although he quit writing for a time, partly as a result of this experience, he later published *Tomcat in Love* (1998).

O'Brien settled in the Boston, Massachusetts, area. He has received a variety of awards both for writing—from the Guggenheim Foundation and the National Endowment for the Arts, among others—and for his work with the Vietnam Veterans of America.

The Writer's Work

Much of Tim O'Brien's work does not deal explicitly with warfare. However, Vietnam remains the subject matter for which he is best known, and themes dealing with Vietnam appear even in his "nonwar" novels.

Themes in O'Brien's Work. Two themes are especially important in O'Brien's fiction. One concerns the power of the imagination to create fictions that are, paradoxically, truer than literal truth. This happens, O'Brien suggests, because the artist's imagination is able to produce stories allowing the reader to understand truths that rational analysis could never make clear. Moreover, fiction allows the writer to create events that the writer wishes had happened: The dead can be returned to life; quarrels can be reconciled; wrong actions can be examined and explained. This becomes the subject of many nonfiction passages in *The Things They Carried*, and it is the implicit subject of *Going After Cacciato*. O'Brien's later novel *In The Lake of the Woods* takes the issue a step further; it invites the reader to decide what must have happened as the voice of the narrator discusses the implications of the various possibilities.

O'Brien is also interested in courage. He leads the reader away from defining courage simply as a person's willingness to risk physical pain or death. Particularly in *If I Die in A Combat Zone, Box Me Up and Ship Me Home* and *The Things They Carried*, he considers a sort of courage that allows one to take unpopular actions out of moral conviction. O'Brien suggests that such a courage is even more demanding than physical bravery, which leads to action in a rush of adrenaline.

O'Brien discussed this concept of courage particularly in reference to resisters to the war in Vietnam who left the United States to avoid being drafted into a war they considered wrong. Such men stand in contrast to those who allowed themselves to be drafted because they were afraid that public opinion might label them cowards. As it was for Henry Fleming, the young soldier in American novelist Stephen Crane's *The Red Badge of Courage: An Episode of the American Civil War* (1895), the ex-

Alberto Savinio's 1927 work *The Dream of the Poet* evokes the transformative power of the imagination. For O'Brien, the imagination is a mode of transport that affords the writer the freedom to renegotiate his fidelity to what is real.

As O'Brien's work identifies, during the years of the Vietnamese involvement, courage took many forms. In Nguyen Duc Tho's watercolor *Paraded American Prisoner*, a featureless, almost ghostlike figure is subjected to the humiliating taunts of his captors. The fate of some American prisoners of war would never be known.

perience of being under fire is a powerful, and often humiliating, test for soldiers in O'Brien's fiction.

Technique in O'Brien's Work. O'Brien's writing has been compared to that of the American novelist Ernest Hemingway, whose early twentieth-century fiction also considered themes of war and courage. Hemingway's spare, undecorated prose, characterized by declarative sentence structures with little in the way of elaborate description, seems to be echoed in O'Brien's narratives, and O'Brien himself faulted some of his early work for being too "purple" or flowery. Like Hemingway before him, O'Brien creates powerful descriptions with well-chosen verbs and nouns instead of relying upon overused adjectives.

O'Brien enjoys stretching the boundaries of genres, another characteristic of his style. The revised version of *The Things They Carried*, for example, intermixes short stories with memoirs and authorial commentary on the nature of fiction. O'Brien uses similar techniques in *In the Lake of the Woods*.

Characters in O'Brien's Work. Many of O'Brien's characters, especially those of his war fiction, seem closely modeled on people or types he must have observed in life. The members of Paul Berlin's company in *Going After Cacciato*, for instance, seem to resemble the characters in *The Things They Carried* and the nonfiction *If I Die in a Combat Zone, Box Me Up and Ship Me Home*. In contrast, some of O'Brien's other characters—for example, William Cowling in *The Nuclear Age* or Thomas Chippering in *Tomcat in Love*—seem more like literary constructions. O'Brien's female characters have sometimes been faulted for being like

In this 1969 photograph, a soldier glances back as he crawls toward enemy emplacements in the Hiep Duc Valley in South Vietnam. The minds of some of O'Brien's male protagonists have been permanently stamped with memories of the war. Vietnam is a haunted space they never fully left behind.

some of Hemingway's women—more the product of male imagination than of accurate renderings, although Kathy Wade of *In the Lake of the Woods* is well drawn.

Americans in Vietnam. The American experience at war in Vietnam from the years 1961–1973 has been a powerful source of inspiration for Tim O'Brien, even in his work which does not deal explicitly with it. French colonial rule in Vietnam ended in 1954 with the French defeat against Vietnamese nationalist forces in a battle at Dien Bien Phu. Following this battle, an agreement made at an international conference in Geneva, Switzerland, divided Vietnam into North and South until elections could be held. Instead, the elections scheduled for 1956 were canceled by Ngo Dinh Diem, the president of South Vietnam, with the support of the United States.

Communist forces in North Vietnam, led by Ho Chi Minh, had expected to profit from these elections, and conflict between the two sides began to escalate. The United States, fearing the effects of communist rule in an area of strategic importance, supported the government of the South against guerilla attacks by the Viet Cong, a force of insurgents supported by the communist government of the North.

U.S. financial support swiftly escalated to military advisers, and by 1961 American support troops were present in the South. In August 1964, in response to a reported attack on U.S. warships, the United States passed the Gulf of Tonkin Resolution, pledging continued American military support for South Vietnam.

Many Americans began to question the wisdom of the U.S. military commitment in Vietnam. Corruption seemed rampant in South Vietnam; moreover, the number of American casualties was rising while U.S. resources were being drained without evidence of military success. Many believed that American lives and resources were being wasted in another country's civil war. Others, however, believed that the need to halt communism's spread in southeast Asia validated the sacrifices of war. In addition, many Americans felt that questioning the war effort was disloyal to the soldiers who were risking their lives.

Conflict between supporters and antiwar activists escalated throughout the mid-1960s, especially on college and university campuses, where protests were frequent and sometimes violent. By 1968, more than half a million American troops were in Vietnam, along with air and naval units. However, the United States suffered heavy losses in the North Vietnamese Tet Offensive, launched in January 1968.

American distaste for the war grew even more intense when the events that took place at My Lai on March 16, 1968, came to light after a year's cover-up. About 350 Vietnamese civilians, including women, infants, and elderly men, had been shot and their bodies thrown into a ditch during a killing spree by soldiers under the command of First Lieutenant William L. Calley. When the U.S. government was forced to investigate, several men were court-martialed over the affair. In the end, only Calley was punished; however, he served less than five months in prison.

Under President Richard Nixon, American bombing raids against North Vietnam and communist strongholds in Cambodia increased, but at the same time U.S. ground troops were being withdrawn. A peace agreement between the United States and North Vietnam was signed in January 1973, although the fighting continued until South Vietnam collapsed to the North in 1975. The country was reunified the following year.

BIBLIOGRAPHY

Bates, Milton J. "Tim O'Brien's Myth of Courage." *Modern Fiction Studies* 33 (Summer 1987).

Bonn, Maria S. "Can Stories Save Us? Tim O'Brien and the Efficacy of the Text." *Critique: Studies in Contemporary Fiction* 36 (Fall 1994).

Kaplan, Steven. *Understanding Tim O'Brien*. Columbia: University of South Carolina Press, 1995.

King, Rosemary. "O'Brien's 'How to Tell a True War Story.'" *The Explicator* 57 (Spring 1999).

Lee, Don. "About Tim O'Brien." *Ploughshares* 21 (Winter 1995–1996).

Lomperis, Timothy J. *"Reading the Wind": The Literature of the Vietnam War*. Durham, N.C.: Duke University Press, 1987.

Melling, Philip H. *Vietnam in American Literature*. Boston: Twayne Publishers, 1990.

Mort, John. "Booklist Interview: Tim O'Brien." *Booklist* 90 (August 1994).

Naparsteck, Martin. "An Interview with Tim O'Brien." *Contemporary Literature* 32 (Spring 1991).

Robinson, Daniel. "Getting It Right: The Short Fiction of Tim O'Brien." *Critique: Studies in Contemporary Fiction* 40 (Spring 1999).

LONG FICTION

- 1975 Northern Lights
- 1978 Going After Cacciato (revised in 1989)
- 1985 The Nuclear Age
- 1994 In the Lake of the Woods
- 1998 Tomcat in Love

NONFICTION

- 1973 If I Die in a Combat Zone, Box Me Up and Ship Me Home (revised in 1989)
- 1994 "The Vietnam in Me" (The New York Times Magazine, October 2, 1994)

SHORT FICTION

- 1990 The Things They Carried

Reader's Guide to Major Works

GOING AFTER CACCIATO

Genre: Novel
Subgenre: Magic realism
Published: New York, 1978
Time period: Approximately 1969
Setting: Vietnam

Themes and Issues. In *Going After Cacciato*, Tim O'Brien deals with some of his richest subject matter—the war in Vietnam and its effects on the men who must fight it. The subject allows him to examine two themes that he finds especially interesting. The first is courage, both physical and moral, which Paul Berlin finds lacking in himself in equal measure. The second is the power of the imagination to create fictions that define and interpret the truth. Paul Berlin's fantasies of following Cacciato to Paris to bring him back to the war become a means of examining what the war has done to Berlin and to others in his squad and, by extension, to all fighting men.

The Plot. Paul Berlin, a draftee in Vietnam, has the night watch over the bay at Quang Ngai. During his watch, he ruminates on the events that have led to his being there and on another soldier named Cacciato, who has decided to leave the war by walking to Paris. Much of the novel's action takes place in Paul's imagination during this watch as he imagines his squad following Cacciato to bring him back to the war.

Grenade in hand, a U.S. Special Forces trooper charges North Vietnamese assailants as a medic treats a wounded officer who has been struck by a grenade. This 1968 photograph taken at Ha Than was used on the cover of O'Brien's *Going after Cacciato*.

The chapters titled "The Observation Post" call the reader back to the literal events of Paul's watch, but throughout the rest of the novel another reality unfolds.

In his mind, Paul returns again and again to crucial events of his war experience—the murder of Lieutenant Sidney Martin, killed by a hand grenade thrown by his own men; the deaths of Billy Boy Watkins and several other men from the squad; and his own humiliating experience of losing control of his bowels in his terror under fire. O'Brien repeatedly describes certain events to convey how Paul's own understanding grows bit by painful bit.

In Paul's imaginary journey, the squad follows Cacciato, who always remains elusively ahead of the men, through Asia and the Middle East and across Europe to Paris. Along the way the squad picks up a young woman, Sarkin Aung Wan, whom Paul comes to love. She tempts Paul to leave his squad and live with her in Paris.

Once, the squad is captured in a maze of North Vietnamese tunnels and discusses the war with a philosophical North Vietnamese soldier. In Tehran the men watch a beheading and later discuss the brotherhood of the military with an Iranian officer. As they travel, Paul recalls how reluctant he was to go to Vietnam and his fear of firefights. He recalls how Oscar Johnson, the squad's moral leader, made everyone participate in Lieutenant Martin's death by making each man touch the grenade that evidently killed him. Only Cacciato, always passively independent, was unwilling to touch it, until Paul took Cacciato's hand and placed it against the grenade. Paul also thinks about the men from the squad who have been killed. The novel ends at the end of Paul's watch as he rejoins the squad in the early light, and the men speculate about the real Cacciato's chances for success.

Analysis. Imagination, with its power to create and transform, is associated with nighttime and dreaming, so it is no surprise that it is during his night watch that Paul uses imagination to give order and interpretation to the chaotic events of warfare. He recalls his childhood relationship with his father and his longing to make his father proud of him. He considers the horrifying and grotesque deaths suffered by members of his squad and is relieved to remain alive. He thinks of his own role in Lieutenant Sidney Martin's death. His imaginative ruminations allow him to make his own escape from his real-life circumstances. Like Cacciato, he has found a sane way to deal with a mad situation. The narrator's voice at the end of the novel implies that Paul's night journey may have summoned his courage to endure an unendurable situation.

SOURCES FOR FURTHER STUDY

Herzog, Tobey C. "*Going After Cacciato*: The Soldier-Author-Character Seeking Control." *Critique: Studies in Contemporary Fiction* 24 (Winter 1983).

Kaplan, Steven, "*Going After Cacciato*." In *Understanding Tim O'Brien*. Columbia: University of South Carolina Press, 1995.

Slay, Jack, Jr. "A Rumor of War: Another Look at the Observation Post in Tim O'Brien's *Going After Cacciato*." *Critique: Studies in Contemporary Fiction* 41 (Fall 1999).

IN THE LAKE OF THE WOODS
Genre: Novel
Subgenre: Mystery
Published: New York, 1994
Time period: 1986
Setting: Northern Minnesota

Themes and Issues. Reviewers had mixed responses to this unconventional mystery that explores, but never reveals, what happens to the missing Kathy Wade. However, O'Brien did not intend to write a conventional mystery. Instead, the novel investigates, as does much of O'Brien's fiction, issues of warfare, courage, and people under extreme stress. O'Brien blends the story's narrative with events from the court-martial of Lieutenant William L. Calley for the My Lai massacre and with information from other nonfiction sources, often from American history.

The Plot. The fictional lieutenant governor of Minnesota, John Wade, has just been beaten by a landslide in his bid for the U.S. Senate. He had once been the Democrats' golden boy, but his campaign was shattered when a political enemy revealed to the media his participation in the My Lai massacre during the Vietnam War. Now, bankrupt, his political career in ruins, Wade and his adored wife Kathy have retreated to the Lake of the Woods, a huge wilderness lake on the Minnesota-Canada border, to regroup and decide what to do next.

The son of an alcoholic father who committed suicide when Wade was ten, Wade has kept his involvement in the My Lai massacre a secret from his wife and even from himself, blocking out his memories of what happened there, where he was known as "Sorcerer" for his skill at magic tricks. Wade's Vietnam experience, combined with his longing for his father's love, has left him capable of terrible rages.

Kathy is not sorry about Wade's defeat; she has hated her life as a politician's wife. Her love for Wade has been under stress for years. In college, he sometimes stalked her. During his years in politics, he put his career ahead of their relationship and once persuaded her to have an abortion. Kathy once had an affair with a dentist but ended it out of love for her husband.

During their stay at the lake, Kathy disappears. O'Brien includes evidence to support the possibility that Wade murdered her, but he makes it equally possible to believe that Kathy left Wade, or that she met with a mishap in the wilderness, or that the two may have intentionally left their defeat behind to start life anew elsewhere. In the end, Wade also vanishes. The novel chronicles the investigation of the disappearances.

Analysis. As the "Evidence" chapters in the narrative make clear, O'Brien is as interested in inviting the reader to consider what might have happened to the Wades as he is in describing what did happen. These chapters contain not only evidence from the fictional characters but also items from the world of nonfiction, including pieces from the court-martial transcripts of Lieutenant Calley, passages from texts on grief, items about how wives can help their soldier-husbands readjust to civilian life, and even items

Like John Wade in *In the Lake of the Woods*, the soldiers present at the My Lai massacre found their lives forever marked by guilt, suspicion, and unresolved questions of responsibility. In this photograph from March 1998, an honor guard carries the Vietnamese flag to the memorial marking the massacre that claimed the lives of more than 350 Vietnamese civilians.

from texts on American history, including the massacres of Native Americans.

In the last chapter, "Hypothesis," O'Brien speaks to the reader in what seems to be his own voice, as he has done in some earlier footnotes. He offers a possible version of what happened to Wade, imagining him taking off across the lake to meet Kathy somewhere in rural Canada. However, he does not offer the satisfaction of a tidy conclusion, even though he may wish to do so. He cannot, he suggests, because life is not like that: "Because there *is* no end, happy or otherwise. Nothing is fixed, nothing is solved. The facts . . . finally spin off into the void of things missing. . . ."

SOURCES FOR FURTHER STUDY

Franklin, H. Bruce. Review of *In the Lake of the Woods*, by Tim O'Brien. *The Progressive* 58 (December 1994).

Kaplan, Steven. "*In the Lake of the Woods*." In *Understanding Tim O'Brien*. Columbia: University of South Carolina Press, 1995.

Walters, Colin. Review of *In the Lake of the Woods*, by Tim O'Brien. *Insight on the News* 10 (November 7, 1994).

THE THINGS THEY CARRIED

Genre: Short fiction
Subgenre: Short stories and memoirs
Published: New York, 1990
Time period: Around 1969
Setting: Vietnam

Themes and Issues. An unusual combination of fiction and memoir, *The Things They Carried* concerns O'Brien's experiences in Vietnam. Some pieces are short stories, many of which were originally published elsewhere; others are essays concerning warfare, courage, the nature of fiction, and O'Brien's own experience in the war. Many of the chapters have interwoven themes and characters. In the end, it becomes difficult to tell the fiction from the nonfiction, which is part of O'Brien's central point as he considers the role of fiction in communicating the truth.

This photograph, taken by photographer Larry Burrows for *Life* magazine, captures a U.S. soldier carrying a rocket launcher across a stream during the conflict with North Vietnamese troops in 1966. The title story from *The Things They Carried* starts literally with the heft of a grenade launcher, eventually moving on to the abstract, emotional weight that bogs the soldiers down.

The Plot. The opening story, "The Things They Carried," one of the longest in the collection, introduces certain recurrent characters and themes. Its narrator assumes an objective tone, detailing the various pieces of equipment carried by the soldiers—for example, a grenade launcher, which weighs six pounds unloaded. The narrator goes on to include other items the soldiers carried—photographs, love letters, good-luck charms, drugs, guilt, hope, fear. First Lieutenant Jimmy Cross carries a load of guilt for having allowed romantic fantasies to distract him from his men's safety, resulting in the death of Ted Lavinder. Rat Kiley, the medic, carries emergency medical supplies including a load of M&M's candy. Kiowa, a devout Baptist, carries a Bible that is later retrieved when he dies in a field of human excrement.

In "On the Rainy River," O'Brien relates an apparently nonfiction account of his temptation to dodge the draft by going to Canada. He said, however, that the narrative is entirely fictional and is intended to convey the conflict he felt when he received his draft notice. "Field Trip" describes O'Brien's return visit to Vietnam with his ten-year-old daughter. "The Lives of the Dead" combines the story of how the platoon dealt with war dead; with that of Linda, the narrator's first love, who died of cancer at the age of ten; and of his pain and confusion at losing her. "Ambush" relates how the narrator killed a man.

Analysis. A key chapter in this collection is "How to Tell a True War Story," which blurs the edges between fiction and nonfiction as the narrator relates a story ostensibly told to him by someone who then confesses to having fabricated many details. Metafiction, fiction about writing fiction, invites one to consider the relationship between reader and author. Because the author Tim O'Brien shares many experiences with the narrator of his work, the reader may be tempted to assume that narrator and author are identical, but O'Brien warns against this assumption, just as he warns against jumping to conclusions about the stories' meanings. "Often in a true war story there is not even a point, or else the point doesn't hit you until twenty years later, in your sleep, and you wake up and shake your wife and start telling the story to her, except when you get to the end you've forgotten the point again."

SOURCES FOR FURTHER STUDY

Calloway, Catherine. "'How to Tell a True War Story': Metafiction in *The Things They Carried*." *Critique: Studies in Contemporary Fiction* 36 (Summer 1995).

Chen, Tina. "Unraveling the Deeper Meaning: Exile and the Embodied Poetics of Displacement in Tim O'Brien's *The Things They Carried*." *Contemporary Literature* 39 (Spring 1998).

Kaplan, Steven. "The Undying Uncertainty of the Narrator in Tim O'Brien's *The Things They Carried*." *Critique: Studies in Contemporary Fiction* 35 (Fall 1993).

Other Works

IF I DIE IN A COMBAT ZONE, BOX ME UP AND SHIP ME HOME (1973).

This early collection of nonfiction prose pieces describes Tim O'Brien's experience as a draftee in Vietnam between 1968 and 1970, including his basic training and descriptions of his pre-military life. The collection is interesting on several counts. For readers of O'Brien's Vietnam fiction, this book can be seen as a foundation for characters and events in *Going After Cacciato* and *The Things They Carried*. Characters from the squad, events involving My Lai, and other episodes of violence are represented here as memoir.

This volume also introduces some of O'Brien's concerns with courage, portrayed here in various ways. One type of courage is discussed in O'Brien's aborted attempt to leave the Army for Canada during basic training. He drops his plan mostly because he cannot bear to consider how his actions would appear to his family and their community. Later, O'Brien portrays officers, such as "Mad Mark," who demonstrates a perfect calm in times of intense danger, or the truly mad Major Callicles, for whom courage is a daredevil business that risks others' lives unnecessarily. Courage seems best represented by Captain Johanson, who combines physical bravery with moral courage.

O'Brien records many episodes of violence and atrocities such as the My Lai massacre. Although he never disguises his distaste for a war he thought useless, it is noteworthy that he treats most of his fellow soldiers with respect and compassion, reserving censure only for those who were needlessly brutal.

THE NUCLEAR AGE (1985).

This novel is the story of Thomas Cowling, whose childhood terror of nuclear warfare led to his violent antiwar protest activities, and at last to a private effort to protect his family by digging an enormous bomb shelter in his backyard. Much of the novel chronicles Cowling's career as an antiwar protester, where he works in an underground network with a group of friends he collected during his college days. The most extreme of these is his girlfriend, Sarah, a former cheerleader who sees the similarities between cheerleading and political rhetoric.

Ultimately, however, Cowling drops out of the movement. Training for violent resistance in Cuba has shown him that he has no stomach for physical danger. Finally he breaks off his affair with Sarah, leaves the movement, makes a fortune in uranium, and marries Bobbi, a poet-turned-flight-attendant whose interest in Cowling seems as casual as Sarah's was intense. Cowling recalls this history while digging the bomb shelter for Bobbi and their daughter, Melinda. Bobbi thinks the project is insane, so Cowling locks her and Melinda in their bedroom and nails the door shut while he spends his days digging.

Despite his behavior, Cowling insists that he is not insane. In fact, the ambiguities in Cowling's behavior recall similar ambiguities in John Wade's actions in *In the Lake of the Woods*. On one level, the novel invites the reader to see a perfect sanity in trying to escape the madness of nuclear war. On the other hand, Cowling seems so disengaged from the world that it is difficult to take him seriously, a problem noted by some of the novel's reviewers.

TOMCAT IN LOVE (1998).

Thomas Chippering tells his story in *Tomcat in Love*, O'Brien's first venture into comic writing. Chippering, a professor of linguistics, wants to win back the af-

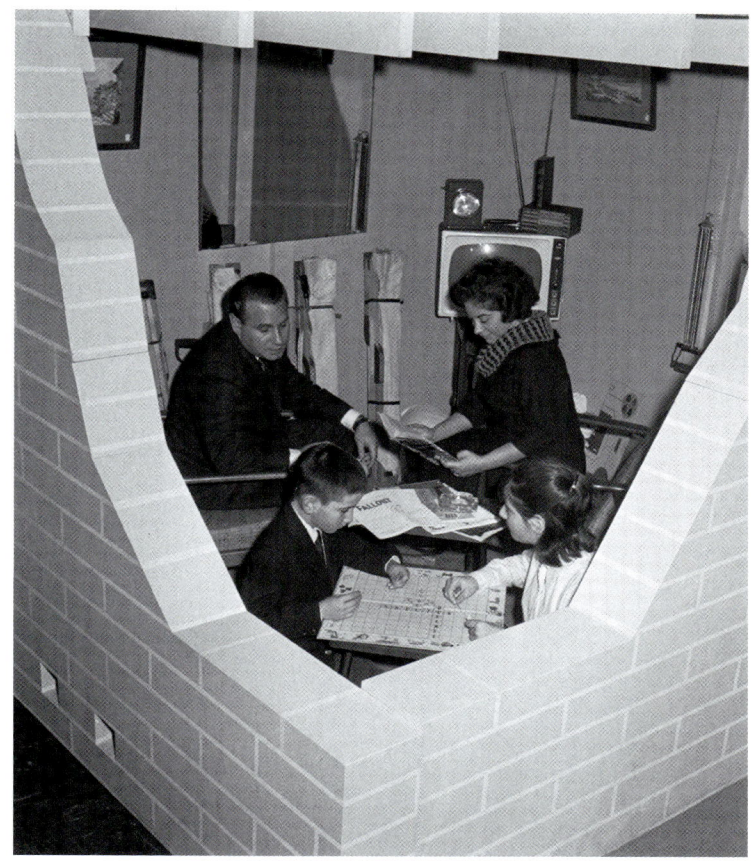

The paranoia and fear engendered by the atomic era find their voice in *The Nuclear Age*'s Thomas Cowling. This photograph from the 1960s shows a bomb shelter a family had constructed in their basement, decked out with all the comforts of home, where they could hide out in the event of nuclear war.

fections of his ex-wife, Lorna Sue, or at least to punish her by breaking up her new marriage in the most spectacular way. Lorna Sue evidently left him because of his incessant womanizing, documented in his categorized and cross-referenced ledger of various conquests. Chippering is aided in his venture by Mrs. Robert Kooshof, to whom he turns for help when he is stranded in her backyard after attempting to spy on his ex-wife's family.

However, the reader learns that things are not exactly as they seem. Chippering's romantic escapades exist mostly in his mind and his ledger. His anger at Lorna Sue borders on paranoia, evidenced by his accusation of her incest with her brother, a childhood friend of his. Mrs. Robert Kooshof, whose first name Chippering is too self-centered to bother learning, offers much more devotion than the fickle Lorna Sue as Chippering finally realizes at the novel's end.

The novel bears on Vietnam in two ways. First, a significant episode in Chippering's Vietnam experience plays a role in his intended revenge on Lorna Sue. Moreover, Chippering himself seems like a metaphor for the escalating U.S. involvement in that war, allowing his sense of injured merit and self-involvement to drag him further and further into a quagmire that logic should have told him long ago to abandon. Eventually Thomas Chippering gets the message.

Resources

A number of Internet sites offer students access to information about Vietnam, both about the war and about the country since the war ended. Many include photos. Such background is useful for readers of Tim O'Brien's Vietnam works. His story "Sweetheart of the Song Tra Bong" was made into a film, *A Soldier's Sweetheart*, by Paramount for Showtime Networks, directed by Thomas Michael Donnelly. Other sources of interest for students of Tim O'Brien include the following:

Tim O'Brien's Home Page. This home page contains selections from O'Brien's novels as well as links to other Vietnam Web sites, a link to an audio clip of a National Public Radio interview with O'Brien concerning *Tomcat in Love*, and a calendar of his reading appearances. (http://www.illyria.com/tobhp.html)

Vets with a Mission. This organization of Vietnam veterans sponsors projects to promote peace and healing in the country in which they fought. The Web site includes a photo album and several useful essays on the history of the country and the war. (http://web20.mindlink.net/vets/)

Writing Vietnam. In April of 1999, Brown University hosted a writing conference on Vietnam for which Tim O'Brien delivered the keynote address. The text of the address as well as a RealAudio recording are available at this site, along with information about other writers who deal with Vietnam and related topics. (http://mama.stg.brown.edu/projects/WritingVietnam/intro.html)

ANN D. GARBETT

Flannery O'Connor

BORN: March 25, 1925, Savannah, Georgia
DIED: August 3, 1964, Milledgeville, Georgia
IDENTIFICATION: Mid-twentieth-century Georgia author best known for her short fiction informed by Christian theology and set in the Protestant South.

Flannery O'Connor's fiction has been lauded for its irony, humor, and symbolism. Often compared to William Faulkner, O'Connor is considered one of the most important short-story writers in American literature. Her thirty-one short stories include "The Life You Save May Be Your Own," "A Circle of Fire," "Greenleaf," "Everything That Rises Must Converge," and "Revelation," all of which won O. Henry Awards. Published posthumously in 1971, *The Complete Stories* won the National Book Award for Fiction. She also published two novels, *Wise Blood* (1952) and *The Violent Bear It Away* (1960), as well as essays and book reviews. By the end of the twentieth century, O'Connor's work was still taught in college literature courses and read by literary critics, theologians, and general readers.

The Writer's Life

The only child of Regina Cline and Edward Francis O'Connor, Jr., Mary Flannery O'Connor was born in Savannah, Georgia, on March 25, 1925. Her father worked in real estate and construction until 1938, when the family moved to Atlanta. He was diagnosed with lupus erythematosus, and, in the fall of 1938, three years before his death, the family moved to Andalusia, the Cline homestead in Milledgeville, Georgia. Until the end of her life, O'Connor lived in Milledgeville, except for a few years when she attended graduate school in Iowa and lived in New York and Connecticut.

Childhood. Despite the tragedy of her father's death in 1941, O'Connor enjoyed a relatively happy childhood. As early as her teenage years, she knew that she wanted to become a writer. She read the works of Nathaniel Hawthorne, whose themes of sin and redemption later influenced her work. The poems and short stories of Edgar Allan Poe also influenced her. O'Connor drew from Poe's use of violence, the macabre, and the grotesque in her own short stories.

O'Connor's life in Milledgeville also shaped her as a writer. Her mother's family included members of the southern gentry, a class of people that appears frequently in O'Connor's fiction. Regina O'Connor had both a deep sense of her family's privileged place in the social hierarchy of the South and a modern, southern middle-class viewpoint. O'Connor portrays and parodies both in her work. Milledgeville was the site of the state prison, as well as the state mental hospital. The presence of these institutions in the community may have heightened O'Connor's awareness of the inherent violence and self-destructiveness of human nature, themes that dominate her fiction.

Education. O'Connor graduated from the Peabody High School in 1942 and entered Georgia State College for Women (now Georgia College) in Milledgeville. During college and high school she drew satiric cartoons for student newspapers, which helped her develop her comic skills and use of exaggeration. She graduated from college

O'Connor expressed an interest in books at an early age. This photograph of O'Connor, taken in the late 1920s, conveys an intensity that is evident in her later works.

Students from Georgia State College for Women, O'Connor's alma mater, pose for a photograph in 1933, about nine years before O'Connor entered the Milledgeville, Georgia, school. These students were from the last class to wear uniforms on campus. O'Connor would later explore societal changes and the decline of long-standing southern culture in her fiction.

in June, 1945, with a bachelor's degree in sociology and English. Her talent for writing fiction won her a scholarship to the University of Iowa, where she earned a master of fine arts degree in creative writing in 1947. During her tenure at the university, she published "The Geranium," her first short story, which appeared in *Accent* in 1946. She later enrolled in the prestigious Writer's Workshop at the university and, in 1948, was invited to Yaddo, an artists' colony in Saratoga Springs, New York.

Artist in Transition. O'Connor's brief tenure at Yaddo put her in contact with celebrated writers and editors, including poet and Roman Catholic convert Robert Lowell and Robert Giroux, editor in chief at Harcourt, Brace in New York City. Her stay at the colony was cut short by a controversy surrounding Agnes Smedley, who was accused of being a member of the Communist Party.

O'Connor returned to Milledgeville for a few weeks and continued to work on her novel *Wise Blood*. However, because she felt isolated from the Roman Catholic intellectuals who had befriended her and because she wanted to be closer to the hub of the publishing world, she moved back to New York in 1949. When she discovered that city life did not agree with her, she accepted an invitation to live in Ridgefield, Connecticut, with Robert and Sally Fitzgerald. Both husband and wife had ties to the literary world. Robert was a classics scholar and had translated many classical works, including the *Odyssey* and *Iliad* of Homer (ca. 800 b.c.e.) and the *Aeneid* of Vergil (ca. 29–19 b.c.e.) Sally later edited *The Habit of Being: Letters* (1979), a collection of O'Connor's letters. During her time with the Fitzgeralds, O'Connor completed the manuscript of *Wise Blood* in 1950 and was offered a contract by Giroux.

Just as her career was beginning to blossom, O'Connor suffered her first attack of disseminated lupus erythematosus. She was on her way to Milledgeville before Christmas, 1950, when she became ill. At first the doctors diagnosed her as having acute rheumatoid arthritis, but they later discovered that she was suffering

The fanfare of peacock plumage would have been a regular sight to O'Connor, who owned several peacocks and was notorious for her love of peafowl.

from the same disease that had killed her father nearly ten years earlier. She returned briefly to Connecticut but then moved back to the family dairy farm in Milledgeville, where her mother lived.

Life at Home. *Wise Blood* was published to critical acclaim in 1952, and from her home O'Connor kept in touch with her friends, her readers, and the editors at Farrar and Giroux. O'Connor wrote three hours a day in the mornings and then rested until two in the afternoon, when she received guests. Far from being a recluse, she enjoyed having visitors and giving small parties. She was known for her love of peafowl and kept several peacocks as pets. When her health permitted, O'Connor traveled to colleges and universities to do readings and receive honorary degrees. Once she traveled to Europe to seek a cure for her disease at Lourdes, France.

In 1953, after winning *The Kenyon Review* Fellowship in fiction, she began to write a collection of short stories, entitled *A Good Man Is Hard to Find* and published in 1955. In 1958 she began work on *The Violent Bear It Away*, which was published in 1960. From 1963 to 1964, she worked on *Everything That Rises Must Converge*, a collection of short stories that was published posthumously in 1965.

Final Illness. Throughout 1963 O'Connor became increasingly weak and suffered fainting spells. Around Christmastime, she was diagnosed with and treated for anemia. Her letters reveal that she sensed something was wrong, and she concentrated on writing what would be her last short-story collection. In February 1964 she learned that she would need surgery for a benign fibroid tumor. Her physician was concerned that an operation would activate her lupus, which had been controlled for years by cortisone and other drugs. She had the surgery, which did reactivate her lupus. As the months passed, she continued to work on her fiction, but because of her deteriorating condition, her progress was slow. She died of kidney failure in Milledgeville on August 3, 1964.

HIGHLIGHTS IN O'CONNOR'S LIFE

1925 Mary Flannery O'Connor is born on March 25 in Savannah, Georgia.
1938 O'Connor's family moves from Savannah to Milledgeville, Georgia.
1941 Father dies of lupus erythematosus.
1942 O'Connor graduates from Peabody High School.
1945 Graduates from Georgia State College for Women in Milledgeville with a bachelor's degree.
1946 Publishes first short story, "The Geranium," in *Accent*.
1947 Receives master of fine arts degree from University of Iowa.
1948 Resides at Yaddo, a writers' colony in Saratoga Springs, New York.
1950 Has first episode of what is later diagnosed as lupus erythematosus.
1951 Moves to Andalusia, the Cline family dairy farm near Milledgeville, with mother; convalesces and raises peafowl.
1952 Publishes *Wise Blood*.
1953 Receives *The Kenyon Review* Fellowship in fiction.
1954 Is reappointed a Kenyon Fellow.
1955 Publishes *A Good Man Is Hard to Find*.
1957 Receives grant from the National Institute of Arts and Letters; wins O. Henry Award for "Greenleaf."
1959 Receives Ford Foundation Grant.
1960 Publishes *The Violent Bear It Away*.
1962 Reissues *Wise Blood* with author's note; is awarded honorary doctorate from St. Mary's College.
1963 Wins O. Henry Award for "Everything That Rises Must Converge"; is awarded honorary degree from Smith College.
1964 Dies of kidney failure on August 3 in Milledgeville, Georgia.
1965 Short-story collection *Everything That Rises Must Converge* is published posthumously; short story "Revelation" is awarded posthumous O. Henry Award.
1971 *The Complete Stories* is published posthumously and wins National Book Award.
1985 *Flannery O'Connor's Library: Resources of Being* is published posthumously.

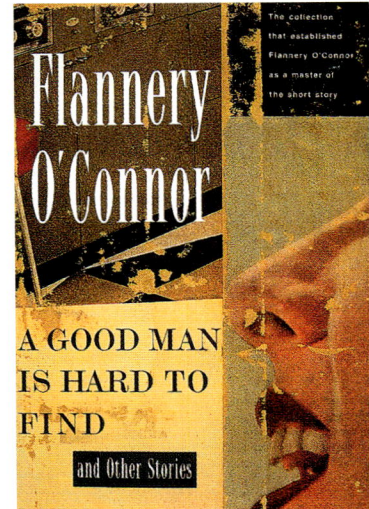

The Writer's Work

Flannery O'Connor published short stories, two novels, and nonfiction, but she is primarily known for her short fiction. Most of her stories portray psychologically and spiritually tormented people who are from the backwoods and small towns of the American South. She uses her bizarre characters and their harsh environments to comment on contemporary Christians' loss of spiritual consciousness and lukewarm commitment to their faith.

Issues in O'Connor's Fiction. A Roman Catholic, O'Connor viewed life through the lens of her faith. Her point of view was in direct opposition to the increased materialism and rationalist doctrine that were gaining a foothold in the society of her time. From a theological perspective, rationalist thought reflects the belief that human beings can discern spiritual truth without the aid of divine revelation and that reason alone can determine moral be-

Horace Pippin's 1945 oil painting *Holy Mountain III* (Hirshhorn Museum and Sculpture Garden, Smithsonian Institution, Washington, D.C.) depicts the artist's profound hope for peace and brotherhood and the end of racism, symbolized by the biblical lion and lamb lying down together. The painting reflects the religious undertones in O'Connor's work and embraces her wish for peace and equality.

Robert Gwathmey's 1965 painting *Belle* illustrates many of the southern stereotypes found in O'Connor's writing. On the right we have the southern belle in hair curlers, the racist, and the preacher, while on the left we see the opportunist and exhibitionist reminiscent of the con man Hoover Shoats and his sidekick, Solace Layfield, in *Wise Blood*, and the slouched figure on the far left evokes the bewilderment of Frank in *The Violent Bear It Away*.

havior. O'Connor saw both materialism and rationalism as threats to religious belief because, in her view, they dulled the need for faith and redemption.

O'Connor also explored societal changes that were taking place in the 1950s and 1960s. She recognized that many aspects of traditional southern culture had long been in decline. Many of her stories grapple with the issues of racism and civil rights. She died just as the national Civil Rights movement was advancing, but her writings indicate that she was in sympathy with the movement. However, O'Connor also believed that there were traditional southern values derived from religion, education, and government that should be preserved. She believed that these values, combined with those of equality and respect for human dignity espoused by the Civil Rights movement, could transform communities into places that would show concern for all people.

People in O'Connor's Fiction. O'Connor's central characters are of two main types. Her novels' main characters are "Christ-haunted" individuals who are caught between God and the devil and attempt to deny the reality of God. In her short stories, many of the protagonists have false visions of themselves. A violent outside figure or force acts as a vehicle to destroy their self-delusions, bringing about their spiritual transformations.

Hazel Motes of *Wise Blood* and Frances Tarwater of *The Violent Bear It Away* fall into the first category. Both are products of radical southern Christian Fundamentalist backgrounds, against which they rebel. They feel obliged to fulfill their hereditary prophetic callings but attempt to evade doing so. Finally they commit acts of violence, "in which the devil has been the unwilling instrument of grace." These actions open them up to the possibility of redemption, and they must choose either to follow Christ or to reject him.

Among the most memorable protagonists in O'Connor's short stories are the grandmother in "A Good Man Is Hard to Find," Mrs. May in "Greenleaf," and Mrs. Chestny in "Everything That Rises Must Converge." Each woman believes herself a good Christian, considers herself superior to others, and is blinded by pride.

All of them are violently jolted from their self-delusions by unlikely agents of God. These experiences bring about a "moment of grace," in which each woman is presented with a final opportunity for salvation.

O'Connor's characters, often grotesque and bizarre, are representative of people who lived in the South. Her sharp, ironic characterizations are tempered with her compassionate

SOME INSPIRATIONS BEHIND O'CONNOR'S WORK

Flannery O'Connor's fiction was shaped by her uniquely southern sense of place, as well as her perspective on family and social hierarchy. She did most of her writing at Andalusia, her family's homestead in Milledgeville, Georgia. She drew directly on her immediate environment for the material that filled her stories, from the dusty dirt roads and backwoods fanatics to the genteel southern ladies and coarse hired hands.

The elderly women that figure so prominently in O'Connor's work are patterned after her mother, Regina Cline O'Connor. A product of the middle-class southern gentry, Regina was a formidable woman who held onto many of the old ideas concerning social and racial hierarchy. O'Connor was drawn to her mother's vision of the pre-Civil War glory of the South, but she rejected many of the prejudices that went along with it. Her ambivalence toward her mother's attitudes can be seen in her characterizations of people such as Mrs. May and Mrs. Chestny.

Caroline Gordon, a leading Southern writer and teacher of literature and creative writing, was O'Connor's primary mentor. She guided O'Connor in shaping her religious philosophy and commented on every piece O'Connor wrote. O'Connor and Gordon were both of the southern gentry and shared many of the same views concerning religion. However, even though Gordon's influence over O'Connor's work was considerable, O'Connor did not always accept Gordon's criticism and felt free to follow her own artistic instincts.

The home that O'Connor lived in at 311 West Greene Street in Milledgeville, Georgia, is emblematic of the southern sense of place found in O'Connor's writing. The house was built around 1820 by a U.S. general. It was later leased as a residence for the governor while the Governor's Mansion was under construction. The solid hand-carved columns and the lattice brickwork are representative of the southern pride in fine masonry that existed in the region in the early 1800s.

awareness of the fallen nature of humanity, which she believed could only be healed by acceptance of Christ's sacrifice on the cross.

O'Connor's Literary Legacy. Although O'Connor died when she was just thirty-nine, her influence on American literature is considerable. Her short stories especially have earned her the appreciation of critics and are taught as part of American literature courses in high schools and colleges. Her Christian understanding of sin and redemption has been compared to similar interpretations found in the works of Nathaniel Hawthorne and John Updike.

O'Connor's unique Christian vision grips both critics and general readers, even those who do not share her beliefs. It is ironic that some of the harshest criticism of her work comes from Catholics who sometimes view her as an outsider. However, most critics appreciate her for the way she weaves Christian apologetics, the defense of the divine origin and authority of Christianity, into stories about everyday life in the South. It is impossible to tell how her writing would have developed had she not died in 1964, but many believe her passing was a great loss to American literature.

BIBLIOGRAPHY

Brinkmeyer, Robert H. *The Art and Vision of Flannery O'Connor.* Baton Rouge: Louisiana State University Press, 1989.

Di Renzo, Anthony. *American Gargoyles: Flannery O'Connor and the Medieval Grotesque.* Carbondale: Southern Illinois University Press, 1993.

Enjolras, Laurence. *Flannery O'Connor's Characters.* Lanham, Md.: University Press of America, 1998.

Getz, Lorine M. *Flannery O'Connor, Literary Theologian: The Habits and Discipline of Being.* Lewiston, N.Y.: Edwin Mellen Press, 2000.

Giannone, Richard. *Flannery O'Connor: Hermit Novelist.* Urbana: University of Illinois Press, 2000.

Johansen, Ruthann K. *The Narrative Secret of Flannery O'Connor: The Trickster as Interpreter.* Tuscaloosa: University of Alabama Press, 1994.

McMullen, Joanne H. *Writing Against God: Language as Message in the Literature of Flannery O'Connor.* Macon, Ga.: Mercer University Press, 1996.

Orvell, Miles. *Flannery O'Connor: An Introduction.* Jackson: University of Mississippi Press, 1991.

Quinn, John J., ed. *Flannery O'Connor: A Memorial.* Scranton, Pa.: University of Scranton Press, 1995.

Spivey, Ted R. *Flannery O'Connor: The Woman, the Thinker, the Visionary.* Macon, Ga.: Mercer University Press, 1995.

SHORT FICTION

Year	Title
1955	A Good Man Is Hard to Find
1955	"Good Country People"
1964	"Revelation"
1965	Everything That Rises Must Converge
1971	The Complete Stories

LONG FICTION

Year	Title
1952	Wise Blood
1960	The Violent Bear It Away

NONFICTION

Year	Title
1969	Mystery and Manners
1979	The Habit of Being: Letters, ed. Sally Fitzgerald
1983	The Presence of Grace
1986	The Correspondence of Flannery O'Connor and Brainard Cheneys

MISCELLANEOUS

Year	Title
1988	Collected Works

Reader's Guide to Major Works

THE VIOLENT BEAR IT AWAY
Genre: Novel
Subgenre: Tragicomic realism
Published: New York, 1960
Time period: 1950s
Setting: Powderhead, a backwoods homestead; unnamed southern city

Themes and Issues. Flannery O'Connor took the title of her second novel from the Bible's Matthew 11:12: "From the days of John the Baptist until now, the kingdom of heaven suffereth violence, and the violent bear it away." Like *Wise Blood*, which preceded it, *The Violent Bear It Away* reflects a Christian Fundamentalist perspective. However, in this book, the fierceness of the Fundamentalist vision is even more apparent. O'Connor demonstrates that the distorted, single-minded, willful view of Christian Fundamentalists is necessary to the struggle for salvation, because only those who are wholly committed to Christ have the power to break through the rationalism, complacency, and materialism that enslave ordinary people.

The central characters are Mason Tarwater, a prophet and preacher; Frank Tarwater, his grandnephew and successor; George Rayber, Mason's nephew and Frank's uncle; and Bishop, George's mentally retarded son. The action in the novel revolves around Mason's charge to Frank that he baptize Bishop, using whatever means he must to accomplish his mission.

The Plot. Mason and his fourteen-year-old grandnephew, Frank, live in Powderhead, a backwoods refuge located near a large southern city. Mason is an uncompromising preacher who believes that he is called by God to be a prophet, and he has groomed Frank to take his place after his death.

It is not the first time the old man has tried to indoctrinate one of his relatives into the Christian faith. Years before, he kidnapped his seven-year-old nephew George and brought him to Powderhead to baptize him. Mason accomplished his mission, but George's parents

Rebecca Davenport's 1982 oil painting *Sommers: Kettleburn* embodies the southern backwoods lifestyle that permeates much of O'Connor's work. Here, the adult male figure, much like Mason in O'Connor's novel *The Violent Bear It Away*, appears to shield the child from the influence of outside forces. Davenport has said of her paintings, "I try to portray my subjects' ugliness and their beauty, their honesty and their self-deception through my knowledge of them and through an exploration of myself." The writing of Flannery O'Connor has been a major influence in her work.

arrived at Powderhead and demanded the return of their son. When George grows up, he becomes a schoolteacher, turning his back on religious faith and embracing rationalism.

Frank is the son of George's sister, who was killed in a car crash. George wants to care for the infant Frank and educate him to become a rationalist like himself, but Mason wants to bring up the boy to become a preacher. Finally, Mason kidnaps Frank, just as he kidnapped George years before. When George comes to retrieve the child, Mason shoots at him, nicking his ear and making him partially deaf. Eventually George marries, and his son, Bishop, is born.

When the story opens, Mason is stricken while sitting at the breakfast table and dies. Before his death, the older man forced his grandnephew to promise that when he died, the boy would bury him properly and place a cross above the grave. Resentful of the control that his great-uncle held over him, Frank reluctantly begins to dig a grave. As he does so, he hears a voice in his head—the voice of reason—urging him to take the easy way out and burn the body. Later, under cover of darkness, Frank sets fire to the house, believing the body is inside. However, a neighbor had already buried the body when Frank was absent from the house.

Frank travels to the city to find George, his only living relative. George greets Frank with pleasure, realizing that he now has the chance to strip the boy of his extreme religious views and educate him as a rationalist, something he could never do with his own son. To this end, George decides to expose Frank to life in the city. George, Bishop, and Frank tour the city for four days, and except for a notice advertising a Pentecostal revival, Frank is uninterested in anything his uncle shows him.

Shortly afterward, Frank escapes George's house to attend the revival. An evangelist preaches powerfully. The event is a turning point for Frank, and even though he resists his great-uncle's command to become a preacher, he knows he must baptize Bishop.

George makes arrangements to take the boys to a lodge located near Powderhead, hoping that if he takes Frank back to the scene of the fire, the shock will release him from his religious obsession. During their stay at the lodge, a bond forms between Bishop and Frank that George can neither fathom nor break. Frank and Bishop row out into the middle of the lake and stay well beyond nightfall. Frank baptizes Bishop even as he drowns him, thrusting his cousin into the kingdom of heaven.

Attempting to reach Powderhead, Frank hitches a ride with an effeminate young man, who drugs and then rapes Frank. The encounter shocks Frank into accepting his spiritual legacy. He returns to Powderhead, and in a final surrender to his destiny, receives a fiery vision, which causes him to turn back toward the city to preach to the unsaved.

Analysis. Written ten years after *Wise Blood*, O'Connor's first novel, *The Violent Bear It Away* again portrays a character who tries to escape his prophetic calling. Instead of striving, as Hazel Motes does in *Wise Blood*, against the "counterfeit" faith of competing evangelists, Frank must deal with the force of modern rationalism embodied in George. George's stubborn refusal to acknowledge Christ is symbolized by his deafness and recalls Christ's words in Matthew 13:15: "This is why I speak to them in parables . . . and hearing they hear not, nor do they understand."

The narrative includes other biblical allusions as well. In part 1 of the novel, the relationship between Mason and his young grandnephew is reminiscent of that of Elijah and Elisha. Part 2 depicts Frank trying to resist and escape his calling, much as Jonah did. Part 3 also alludes to the Jonah story, as Frank's visionary experience causes him to turn his face toward his own Nineveh and carry his message to "the dark city, where the children of God lay sleeping."

SOURCES FOR FURTHER STUDY

Baumgaertner, Jill P. *Flannery O'Connor: A Proper Scaring*. Wheaton, Ill.: H. Shaw, 1988.

Friedman, Melvin J., and Beverly L. Clark, eds. *Critical Essays on Flannery O'Connor*. Boston: G. K. Hall, 1985.

Giannone, Richard. *Flannery O'Connor and the Mystery of Love*. Urbana: University of Illinois Press, 1989.

Rath, Sura P., and Mary N. Shaw, eds. *Flannery O'Connor: New Perspectives*. Athens: University of Georgia Press, 1996.

Whitt, Margaret E. *Understanding Flannery O'Connor*. Columbia: University of South Carolina Press, 1995.

WISE BLOOD

Genre: Novel
Subgenre: Tragicomic realism
Published: New York, 1952
Time period: Late 1940s
Setting: Fictional southern city

Themes and Issues. Although O'Connor's short stories deal obliquely with Christian themes, the metaphorical imagery in *Wise Blood* openly portrays a radical Fundamentalist vision. Hazel Motes, the main character, is an ex-soldier from the backwoods of Tennessee who tries to evade his hereditary calling as a preacher, only to discover that he cannot resist the presence of Christ. In an introduction to a 1962 reprint of the novel, O'Connor makes plain her intention to reach those readers who prefer to think that "the life and death belief in Christ . . . is a matter of no great consequence." Although a Roman Catholic, O'Connor reveals her affinity for southern Fundamentalism by bringing Hazel to the point where he must make a choice: either surrender to God or face damnation.

The Plot. Hazel Motes, an intense and belligerent man, travels by train to the city of Taulkinham after being discharged from the service. Originally from Eastrod, a small backwoods Tennessee town, Hazel is as much fleeing from his past as running toward his future. His grandfather was a Fundamentalist preacher who preached the Gospel as he stood on the hood of his Ford automobile. His mother was also a religious woman. They both expected

Thomas Hart Benton's 1932 painting *Arts of the South* captures an array of reactions to the outbursts of the speaker. There are those who play along with the tune, those who humbly coward, and those who appear deaf and blind to the message. As in O'Connor's *Wise Blood*, it is difficult to distinguish the corrupt from the truly pious. In O'Connor's own words, *Wise Blood* explores the "religious consciousness without a religion."

that Hazel would become a preacher, but he rebels, joins the army, and denies his faith. After the death of his relatives and his discharge from the service, Hazel is able to pursue his own destiny.

When he reaches downtown Taulkinham, Hazel meets the blind evangelist Asa Hawks and his young daughter, Sabbath Lilly, who are handing out tracts. At the same time he also becomes acquainted with Enoch Emery, a young man who is new to the area.

Hazel is fascinated by Asa and Sabbath, even though Asa represents everything that Hazel is trying to deny. When Asa tries to convert Hazel, Hazel says that he has founded the Church Without Christ, where "the blind don't see and the lame don't walk and what's dead stays that way."

Hazel buys an old Essex automobile in a junkyard and preaches his godless gospel from the hood of the car, in a perverse parody of his dead grandfather. While living at the same rooming house as Asa and Lilly, Hazel discovers that Asa is not really blind and is stunned to learn that Asa has been living a lie. Hazel's disillusionment only strengthens his resolve to promote the Church Without Christ.

When Asa leaves town, Sabbath Lilly and Hazel begin to live together. Enoch, wanting to win Hazel's friendship, steals a sand-filled mummified man from a local museum, which he calls a "new jesus." After Enoch delivers his gift to Hazel's room, Sabbath Lilly cradles it in her arms in a grotesque parody of the Madonna and Child. Hazel, disgusted, resolves to abandon Sabbath Lilly and move on to a new city to preach his own brand of truth.

On his way out of town, Hazel encounters the con man Hoover Shoats and his sidekick, Solace Layfield, who resembles Hazel in both dress and physique. Shoats has heard Hazel preach, and in imitation of him, Shoats founded the Holy Church of Christ Without Christ. Shoats hired Layfield to be his "prophet." Layfield is dressed exactly like Hazel, which angers Hazel. He follows Layfield home and demands that Layfield strip off his clothes. Then Hazel brutally murders him. Hazel's violent act is the beginning of his redemption. He heads back to Taulkinham, stops at a hardware store to pick up some lime, goes to his old rooming house, and blinds himself.

Hazel's blinding is a spiritual turning point. At last he is able to "see" clearly and surrender to Christ. He lives the life of an ascetic, wearing barbed wire around his chest and filling his shoes with rocks and glass to atone for his sins. His landlady, Mrs. Flood, is drawn to him and proposes marriage. Hazel again flees the rooming house. When he is gone for two days, Mrs. Flood reports him missing, only to discover that he has died in a ditch.

Analysis. *Wise Blood* is notable for its ironic portrayals of true piety versus counterfeit faith, of the consequences and benefits of personal and spiritual isolation, and of the advantages of physical blindness as a means to spiritual insight. Clarity of vision is a major theme in *Wise Blood*, as is evidenced by O'Connor's choice of name for her main character. "Haze" symbolizes Hazel's clouded spiritual vision, while "Motes" refers to Matthew 7:3: "And why beholdest thou the mote that is in thy brother's eye, but considerest not the beam that is in thine own eye." Other distinguishing elements of the novel are the grotesque characterizations and the nightmarish settings, which serve to highlight Hazel's religious conflict.

Many consider *Wise Blood* O'Connor's best work. However, when it was first published in 1952, the novel was greeted with shock and misunderstanding. O'Connor's use of exaggeration, distortion, and violence both challenged and repelled critics. Over time, readers came to appreciate the book's profound spiritual and psychological insight. In 1979 *Wise Blood* was made into a film directed by John Huston.

SOURCES FOR FURTHER STUDY
Baumgaertner, Jill P. *Flannery O'Connor: A Proper Scaring*. Wheaton, Ill.: H. Shaw, 1988.

Bloom, Harold, ed. *Flannery O'Connor*. New York: Chelsea House, 1986.

Edmunds, Susan. "Through a Glass Darkly: Visions of Integrated Community in Flannery O'Connor's *Wise Blood*." *Contemporary Literature* 37, no. 4 (Winter 1996): 559–595.

Kreyling, Michael, ed. *New Essays on "Wise Blood."* New York: Cambridge University Press, 1995.

Rath, Sura P., and Mary N. Shaw, eds. *Flannery O'Connor: New Perspectives*. Athens: University of Georgia Press, 1996.

Whitt, Margaret E. *Understanding Flannery O'Connor*. Columbia: University of South Carolina Press, 1995.

Other Works

"THE ARTIFICIAL NIGGER" (1955). One of Flannery O'Connor's favorite stories, "The Artificial Nigger" is about the initiation of a young boy into the world of experience by his grandfather. As in many coming-of-age stories, the narrative revolves around a journey. Mr. Head decides to take his grandson, Nelson, to Atlanta by train in order to show him the complexities of city life. He also warns Nelson against black people.

When they first reach Atlanta, Nelson and Head weigh themselves on a coin-operated scale in front of a store. The machine spits out a fortune card for Nelson that reads: "You have a great destiny ahead of you but beware of dark women." As their journey progresses, the master/disciple relationship between Head and Nelson deteriorates. They meet a black woman whom Nelson finds compelling because of her sensuality. Remembering Head's admonitions against "niggers," Nelson decides to trust Head's judgment. Subsequently, they become lost. In his confusion, Nelson accidentally knocks down a woman, who then threatens to send Head the doctor's bill. Head denies that Nelson is his boy, and his betrayal causes a rift in their relationship. Finally the two come upon a plaster lawn statue of a black boy. They sense that they "are faced with some great mystery." Their shared wonder bridges the gap between them.

"EVERYTHING THAT RISES MUST CONVERGE" (1961). The title of this story, originally published in 1961 and in book form in 1965, is taken from *The Phenomenon of Man* (1955) by Jesuit philosopher Pierre Teilhard de Chardin. Teilhard used the phrase to refer to spiritual evolution. In her story O'Connor applies Teilhard's phrase to racism, showing how the practice of racial superiority prevents humanity from rising and converging into a unified society. The phrase also relates to the emotional and spiritual growth of Julian, the main character.

Mrs. Chestny, Julian's mother, is a member of the southern gentry. Her family's fortunes declined, and she is now a middle-class woman who has had to scrimp to send her son to college. Although she is not mean or malicious, she has not let go of the pride and racial prejudice of her aristocratic heritage. Julian, on the other hand, fancies himself a liberal thinker. He takes perverse pleasure in attacking his mother's views on race. Yet he does not realize that he suffers from a false sense of intellectual superiority and liberal idealism.

On a bus trip downtown, Julian and Mrs. Chestny encounter a large black woman and her young son. The woman is wearing the same purple hat that Julian's mother is wearing. Julian is delighted, believing that his mother would be horrified to think she had anything in common with a black woman. At first his mother is shocked and then ignores her "black double" as she condescendingly pays attention to the boy.

When they all get off the bus, Mrs. Chestny gives the little boy a penny. The black woman, insulted by Mrs. Chestny's patronizing attitude, hits her with her pocketbook. Julian derides his mother for her foolishness. However, the black woman's attack and Julian's hateful words are too much for her. She suffers a stroke and dies on the sidewalk. Julian falls to his knees in grief, finally seeing himself as he really is—selfish and self-centered. His realization marks a turning point in his spiritual evolution, and he is finally free to rise beyond his self-delusion.

"A GOOD MAN IS HARD TO FIND" (1953). This short story, originally published in 1953 and collected in 1955, is frequently anthologized in high school and college textbooks. It offers an excellent example of one of O'Connor's major themes: that God's grace can transform individuals.

As the story opens, a Georgia family is planning a vacation to Florida. The grandmother wants to go to Tennessee instead because she has heard on the radio that the Misfit, a serial killer, has escaped from prison and is heading toward Florida. The rest of the family ignores her objections, and the next day they drive to Florida. The grandmother persuades her son to take a detour along a dirt road because she swears that she once visited an old plantation situated on that same road.

The car overturns, and the family ends up in a ditch. They are rescued by three men, one of whom the grandmother recognizes as the Misfit. Realizing that the Misfit intends to kill them, she tries to talk him out of it, while his henchmen take the family members into the woods one by one and shoot them. Finally, she is the only one left. In a flash of clarity, she looks beyond the Misfit's twisted nature and sees his humanity. Her moment of grace comes

This undated photograph of O'Connor standing next to a self-portrait reflects her love of peacocks while it also wryly and unwittingly embodies O'Connor's understated message of equality in her short story "Everything that Rises Must Converge," where the presence of a hat is used to reinforce her view that all people are created equally.

when she declares, "Why you're one of my babies. You're one of my own children!" Her compassion initially attracts and then repels him, and he shoots her.

"GREENLEAF" (1956). This is one of O'Connor's more unusual stories because it draws its imagery from both pagan myth and Christian tradition. Mrs. May operates a dairy farm, and Mr. Greenleaf is her hired hand. He has twin sons who are also owners of a prosperous dairy farm. The twins' success irks Mrs. May, because she considers them her social inferiors. One night their bull escapes and appears under Mrs. May's bedroom window, chewing on her hedge. In the moonlight, the bull takes on a godlike aura, resembling Dionysus in his bull form. The image becomes even more striking when a piece of hedge slips around his horns. The garland appears as a "menacingly prickly crown," suggesting a parallel to Christ's sacrifice.

Mrs. May is afraid that the bull will corrupt her purebred cattle. The next day she drives to the twins' farm and demands that they come and get the animal. They do not want the bull back, and Mrs. May realizes that she will have to destroy it herself. She forces Mr. Greenleaf to take her in his truck and to drive after the bull. They come to a tree-ringed pasture that resembles an amphitheater. Mr. Greenleaf goes into the woods with his gun to look for the bull, while Mrs. May waits by the truck. Suddenly the bull rushes toward her and gores her through the heart. At the moment of her death, Mrs. May experiences a blinding revelation—a revelation that dies with her as she slumps over the bull and appears to whisper her intimate secret into his ear.

Resources

The Flannery O'Connor Collection was established in 1946 at the Ida Dillard Russell Library at Georgia College in Milledgeville, Georgia. This center has over six thousand pages of O'Connor's manuscripts, including early drafts of *Wise Blood*, portions of *The Violent Bear It Away*, and most of her short stories. The collection also includes O'Connor's personal collection of more than seven hundred books and journals. Other sources of interest to students of Flannery O'Connor include the following:

Flannery O'Connor Bulletin. This literary journal features literary criticism of Flannery O'Connor's works.(http://www.peacock.gac.peachnut.edu/~sc/focbull.html)

Flannery O'Connor Childhood Home. This nonprofit organization located in Savannah, Georgia, is dedicated to restoring O'Connor's childhood home and maintaining a literary site in her memory. (http://www.ils.unc.edu/flannery/)

Flannery O'Connor Society. Founded in 1992, this is an organization of scholars and researchers interested in exchange of ideas and information about O'Connor's writings. Contact Sura Rath at (srath@pilot.lsus.edu).

PEGGE BOCHYNSKI

Index

Page numbers in **boldface** type indicate article titles. Page numbers in *italic* type indicate illustrations.

Abstentee, The (Moore adaptation of Edgeworth), 1036, 1037, 1038
After the Fall (Miller), 1016, 1019, 1020, 1025, 1028
All My Sons (Miller), 1015, 1016, 1017, 1018, 1019, 1021–22, 1025, 1028
American Appetites (Oates), 1109, 1110, 1111
"Artificial Nigger, The" (O'Connor), 1148
Arts of the South (painting), *1146*

Backus, Stan, *1091*
"Bad Girls" (Oates; short story), 1116
Bad Girls (Oates; play), 1109, 1116–17
Bearden, Romare, *1057*
Belle (painting), *1141*
Bellows, George Wesley, *1109*
Beloved (Morrison), 1049, 1052, 1054, 1056, 1057, 1058, 1059–60, 1062, 1063–65, 1068
Benton, Thomas Hart, *1146*
Black Water (Oates; libretto), 1106, 1107, 1118
Black Water (Oates; novel), 1106, 1107, 1110, 1111, 1116, 1118
Blix (Norris), 1089, 1095
Blonde (Oates), 1106, 1111
Bluest Eye, The (Morrison), 1051, 1052, 1053, 1057, 1058, 1064, 1065
"Boys and Girls" (Munro), 1082–83
Burrows, Larry, *1131*

"Carried Away" (Munro), 1078
Child and Her Mother, Wapato, Yakima Valley, Washington (photograph), *1081*
"Circle of Fire, A" (O'Connor), 1135
Club Night (painting), *1109*
Collected Poems (Moore), 1036, 1037, 1043
Complete Edition of Frank Norris, The, 1090, 1095
Complete Poems of Marianne Moore, The, 1036, 1037, 1041–43
Complete Prose of Marianne Moore, The, 1036, 1043, 1044–46
Complete Stories, The (O'Connor), 1135, 1139, 1143
Cotton Picking, Pulaski County, Arkansas (photograph), *1053*
Creation of the World and Other Business, The (Miller), 1018, 1019, 1025

Crucible, The (Miller), 1015, 1017, 1018, 1019, 1022–24, 1025

Dance of the Happy Shades (Munro), 1071, 1074, 1075, 1080
Davenport, Rebecca, *1144*
Death of a Salesman (Miller), 1013, 1015, 1017, 1018, 1019, 1025–28
Death of a Salesman (poster), *1015*
Double Portrait of the Artist in Time (painting), *1079*
Dragons (mural), *1036*
Dreaming Emmett (Morrison), 1052, 1054, 1064
Dream of the Poet, The (painting), *1124*

Edgeworth, Maria, 1036, 1037
Enemy of the People, An (Miller adaptation of Ibsen), 1015, 1018, 1019, 1025
Ettlinger, Marion, *1074*
Eva Green (Henri), *1050*
"Everything That Rises Must Converge" (O'Connor), 1135, 1139, 1142, 1148–49
Everything That Rises Must Converge (O'Connor), 1138, 1139, 1143, 1148

Fables choisies, mises en vers (Fontaine), 1035, *1036*, 1037, 1046
films, 1015, 1016, 1019, 1020, *1021*, *1023*, *1026*, 1052, 1054, *1063*, 1065, 1066, 1090, 1094, 1096, 1106, *1147*
First Love (Oates), 1109, 1111
Fitzgerald, Sally, 1137
Flannery O'Connor's Library: Resources of Being, 1139
Flurry in Wheat, A (illustration), *1099*
Focus (Miller), 1014, 1017, 1018, 1025
"Four Freedoms, The" (Miller; radio play), 1017, 1018, 1025
Foxfire: Confessions of a Girl Gang (Oates), 1106, 1109, 1111, 1116
Frank Norris of "The Wave" (ed. Lewis), 1090, 1095
"Friend of My Youth" (Munro), 1077

Garner, Margaret, *1059*, *1060*, 1064
Going After Cacciato (O'Brien), 1119, 1122, 1123, 1124, 1125, 1127, 1128–29, 1132

"Good Man Is Hard to Find, A" (O'Connor), 1142, 1149–50
Good Man Is Hard to Find, A (O'Connor), 1138, 1139, 1143
"Granite and Steel" (Moore), 1046
"Greenleaf" (O'Connor), 1135, 1139, 1142, 1150
Gwathmey, Robert, *1141*

Habit of Being, The: Letters (O'Connor; ed. Fitzgerald), 1137, 1143
Hahn, William, *1088*
Harvest Time (painting), *1088*
Henri, Robert, *1050*
Hewitt, Charles, *1017*
Hirsch, Joseph, *1015*
Holy Mountain III (painting), *1140*
"How to Tell a True War Story" (O'Brien), 1132

Ibsen, Henrik, 1015, 1018, 1019, 1021, 1025, 1028
If I Die in a Combat Zone, Box Me Up and Ship Me Home (O'Brien), 1119, 1122, 1123, 1124, 1125, 1127, 1132–33
Impedimenta (painting), *1083*
Incident at Vichy (Miller), 1016, 1018, 1019, 1025
"In Memoriam" (Miller), 1019
In Russia (Miller; photos by Morath), 1018, 1025
In the Lake of the Woods (O'Brien), 1119, 1122, 1123, 1124, 1125, 1126, 1127, 1129–31, 1133
"In the Region of Ice" (Oates), 1104

James, Henry, 1040
Jazz (Morrison), 1052, 1054, 1064, 1068
Johnson, William H., *1065*

"Knife, The" (Moore), 1046

La Fontaine, Jean de, 1035, 1036, 1037, 1046
Lange, Dorothea, *1081*
Lawrence, Jacob, *1045*
Lee-Smith, Hughie, *1077*, *1083*
Lewis, Oscar, 1090, 1095
"Life You Save May Be Your Own, The" (O'Connor), 1135
Li'l Sis (painting), *1065*

Lives of Girls and Women (Munro), 1073, 1074, 1075, 1076, 1077, 1079–80, 1082
Love of a Good Woman, The (Munro), 1075, 1078, 1080
Lundeberg, Helen, *1079*
Lynch, James, *1076*

Man Crazy (Oates), 1109, 1111
Man's Woman, A (Norris), 1089, 1093, 1095, 1101–2
Man Who Had All the Luck, The (Miller), 1014, 1017, 1018, 1025
"Margaret Garner" (engraving), *1059*
Marianne Moore Reader, A, 1036, 1037, 1043
"Marriage" (Moore), 1042–43
Marya: A Life (Oates), 1109, 1111
McTeague (Norris), 1085, 1089, 1093, 1094–97, 1100, 1101, 1102
"Meneseteung" (Munro), 1077
Miller, Arthur, **1013–32**
"Misfits, The" (Miller; short story), 1016, 1018, 1019
Misfits, The (Miller; novel), 1019, 1025
Misfits, The (Miller; screenplay), 1016, 1019, 1025
"Moons of Jupiter, The" (Munro), 1074
Moons of Jupiter, The: Stories (Munro), 1078, 1080
Moore, Marianne, **1033–48**
Moran of the Lady Letty (Norris), 1089, 1090, *1092*, 1093, 1095, 1101
Morath, Ingeborg, 1016, 1018, 1025
Morrison, Toni, **1049–70**
Motley, Archibald, *1055*
"Mouse Metamorphosed into a Maid, The" (Moore), 1046–47
Munch, Edvard, *1117*
Munro, Alice, **1071–84**
My Heart Laid Bare (Oates), 1109, 1110, 1111
Mysteries of Winterthurn (Oates), 1105, 1106, 1109, 1110, 1111, 1112–13

Nast, Thomas, *1097*
New Plays (Oates), 1106, 1111, 1116, 1118
Nobel, Thomas, *1059*
Norris, Frank, **1085–1102**
Northern Lights (O'Brien), 1122, 1123, 1127
Nuclear Age, The (O'Brien), 1122, 1123, 1126, 1127, 1133
Nun with Girl, New Orleans (photograph), *1069*

Oates, Joyce Carol, **1103–18**
O'Brien, Tim, **1119–34**
Observations (Moore), 1035, 1037, 1043
O'Connor, Flannery, **1135–50**
Octopus, An (Moore), 1043
Octopus, The (Norris), 1085, *1088*, 1089, 1090, 1091, 1093, 1095, 1097–98

"Office, The" (Munro), 1074
"On the Rainy River" (O'Brien), 1132
"Open Secrets" (Munro), 1078
Open Secrets: Stories (Munro), 1074, 1078, 1080
O to Be a Dragon (Moore), 1036, 1043
"Ottawa Valley, The" (Munro), 1073
Outside Looking In (painting), *1076*

Pangolin and Other Verse, The (Moore), 1035, 1043
Paraded American Prisoner (watercolor), *1125*
Paradise (Morrison), 1054, 1058, 1064, 1068–69
Patchwork Quilt (painting), *1057*
"Peace of Utrecht, The" (Munro), 1073, 1075, 1077, 1083–84
Perfectionist, The (Oates; play), 1107
Perfectionist and Other Plays, The (Oates), 1106, 1111
Pippin, Horace, *1140*
Pit, The (Norris), 1085, 1089, 1090, 1091, 1095, 1098–1100
Playing in the Dark: Whiteness and the Literary Imagination (Morrison), 1052, 1056, 1064
"Poetry" (Moore), 1041
Price, The (Miller), 1016, 1019, 1025, 1029, 1031
Progress of Love, The (Munro), 1074, 1075, 1078, 1080
Puy, Jean, *1072*

"Red Dress—1946" (Munro), 1077
"Revelation" (O'Connor), 1135, 1139, 1143

Santa Margarita Grade (watercolor), *1091*
Saturday Night (painting), *1055*
"Save the Reaper" (Munro), 1078
Savinio, Alberto, *1124*
Selected Fables of La Fontaine (Moore translation), 1036, 1037, 1043, 1046
Selected Poems (Moore), 1035, 1037, 1043
Shahn, Ben, *1053*
"Something I've Been Meaning to Tell You" (Munro), 1084
Something I've Been Meaning to Tell You: Thirteen Stories (Munro), 1074, 1078, 1080
Sommers: Kettleburn (painting), *1144*
Song of Solomon (Morrison), 1051, 1052, 1053, 1057, 1058, 1064, 1066–68
Soyer, Moses, *1044*
Stella, Joseph, *1030*
Strike (painting), *1045*
Study or The Schoolgirl (painting), *1072*
Sula (Morrison), 1052, 1053, 1057, 1058, 1064, 1069–70

Summer Night on the Beach, A (painting), *1117*
Sunday Dinner (Oates), 1107, 1111

Tar Baby (Morrison), 1052, 1053, 1057, 1058, 1064, 1070
"Tell Me, Tell Me" (Moore), 1047–48
Tell Me, Tell Me (Moore), 1036, 1043
That They May Win (Miller), 1017, 1025
them (Oates), 1103, 1105, 1107, 1109, 1111, 1113–15
"They Too Arise" (Miller), 1014, 1018
"Things They Carried, The" (O'Brien), 1132
Things They Carried, The (O'Brien), 1119, 1122, 1123, 1124, 1125, 1127, 1131–32
Tho, Nguyen Duc, *1125*
Three Plays (Oates), 1106, 1111
Timebends: A Life (Miller), 1013, 1018, 1025
"Timmy" (O'Brien), 1121
"To a Snail" (Moore), 1048
Tomcat in Love (O'Brien), 1119, 1123, 1126, 1127, 1133–34
Twelve Plays (Oates), 1106, 1111
Two Girls (painting), *1077*

Ulmann, Doris, *1069*

Vandover and the Brute (Norris), 1090, 1093, 1095, 1100–1101
"Vietnam in Me, The" (O'Brien), 1123, 1127
View from the Bridge, A (Miller), 1025, 1030, 1031
Violent Bear It Away, The (O'Connor), 1135, 1138, 1139, 1141–42, 1143, 1144–46
Voice of the City of New York Interpreted, The: The Bridge (painting), *1030*

Wanted, Poster Series No. 17 (painting), *1067*
What Are Years (Moore), 1035, 1037, 1043
What I Lived For (Oates), 1103, 1106, 1107, 1109, 1111, 1115–16
White, Charles, *1067*
Who Do You Think You Are? (Munro), 1072, 1073, 1074, 1075, 1080–82
"Wilderness Story, A" (Munro), 1077
Wise Blood (O'Connor), 1135, 1137, 1138, 1139, 1141–42, 1143, 1144, 1145, 1146–48
With Shuddering Fall (Oates), 1104, 1107, 1111
Women in Love (Oates), 1107, 1111
WPA Artists (painting), *1044*

You Must Remember This (Oates), 1109, 1111
Yvernelle: A Tale of Feudal France (Norris), 1088, 1089, 1093, 1095, 1100